The Child Advocacy Handbook

The Child Advocacy Handbook

by Happy Craven Fernandez

The Pilgrim Press
New York

Acknowledgments appear on pages 164-165.

Library of Congress Cataloging in Publication Data

Fernandez, Happy Craven, 1939-
  The child advocacy handbook.

  Includes bibliographical references.
  1. Children's rights—United States. 2. Child welfare—United States. I. Title.
HQ789.F47   323.4'088054   80-24053
ISBN 0-8298-0403-X (pbk.)

The Pilgrim Press, 132 W. 31 Street, New York, New York 10001

Many friends and colleagues have contributed to this book. My thanks to Fran Vandiver who called on the phone in the spring of 1973 and opened a door by asking me to teach a child advocacy course at Temple University. Students in my child advocacy classes have taught me by asking incisive questions and sharing their experiences.

I am indebted to my colleagues in the Parents' Union for Public Schools and in the Powelton-Mantua Educational Fund, who have provided support and expertise in our struggles for quality public schools. All the royalties from this book will be contributed to those organizations and to comparable advocacy groups.

Tony Auth of *The Philadelphia Inquirer* and the other authors who gave their permission to use excerpts from their books have been generous and cooperative.

Honest feedback on the manuscript in its various stages came from friends like Janie Freeman, Shelley Yanoff, Yvonne Hutchins, Mario Howell, Bob Vandiver, Helen Oakes, and Arbutus Sider. Very special thanks to Dick Fernandez who has been a loving critic and a consistent advocate.

And, thank you, John, David, and Richard for frequently reminding me: "But, Mom, aren't you going to *listen* to us—I thought you said children should have a say!"

CONTENTS

INTRODUCTION

We're told to keep our hands off them—except for restraint, but you know teachers hit them all the time. So I reported it but nothing ever happened to them, and now they shun me. I honestly don't know what to do. (an aide in a class for socially and emotionally maladjusted children)

Drugs do keep them quiet—you've got to admit. But some of these kids, only ten and eleven years old, walk around like zombies—nodding off all day. But what can I do? The psychiatrist ordered it. (an attendant in a residential center)

If I had to live in that filthy, cold house, I guess I'd smell and have a snotty nose, too. But if the mother doesn't care and fights anyone who tries to help, it's hopeless. I hate to write off a child that's only seven. (the owner of a corner grocery store)

These hoodlums are taking over our neighborhood. The cops need to get tough on them. Put them away and teach them a thing or two, a little respect. You know it's not safe for me to walk to the grocery store any more. (a seventy-two-year-old retired bricklayer)

I am trying, yes I am. But I can't even keep ahead of the bills. Inflation is killing me—especially food and rent. How can I feed teenage boys when even bread and eggs have tripled in price, and my income stays the same. (the mother of four sons living in an urban area)

Things weren't bad—till Dad got sick. These cancer treatments knock him out for days. Mom is worried sick over him and all the bills. I'm trying to help out—but $2.00 an hour after school doesn't go that far. What more can I do? (a fourteen-year-old who has attempted suicide)

Children have many problems in our society. Many people care, but don't know how to help. The voices of the adults and young people heard above are not exceptions. They illustrate the scope of the problem:

9

—Children are the poorest group in America. Ten million children under eighteen live in poverty. That's more than one in every six.

—Half of all children under fifteen have never been to a dentist.

—One out of every five handicapped children entitled to special education services is not receiving them.

—Cases of child abuse in the home are being reported and treated more often, but no accurate figures exist to measure the actual amount of physical and sexual abuse in homes and institutions.

—Suicides among teenagers have been increasing rapidly and now are the second-ranking cause of death for persons aged fifteen to twenty-five.

—Infant mortality is still very high for such an "advanced" nation. One out of every sixty-five U.S. infants dies.

—Among black and Hispanic children, one out of two drop out of high school.

—Runaways may number a million each year. The average runaway is a fourteen-and-a-half-year-old white Protestant female.[1]

The abuse, violation, and crippling of children's spirits and bodies in homes, prisons, schools and hospitals is graphically described and documented in books like *Throwaway Children, No One Will Listen, Who Speaks for Children?, How Children Fail, Somewhere a Child Is Crying, Crisis in Child Mental Health, Weeping in the Playtime of Others,* and *Children in Jail.* Each is a plea for adults to become advocates for children.

People who care about children—parents, neighbors, and staff persons in schools, day-care centers, juvenile detention centers and health clinics—see the damage being done to our future generation, but often feel helpless and inadequate. What can be done? Does anyone else care? Is it possible to bring about change?

Child advocates care and do cause changes. This book tells how each of us can use our roles to be advocates for children. Some of the questions addressed include: How do children's

rights provide a basis for advocacy? How can a person be effective as a child advocate? What skills does a child advocate need? How can parents and staff persons use power in their roles as advocates? How can advocacy organizations add clout?

This is a resource book for teachers, child-care workers, caseworkers, medical practitioners, staff persons in the agencies and systems that deliver services to children. It is also a resource for parents, grandparents and neighbors who want to be more effective advocates for their own children or for children in their communities.

The focus of this book is on equipping persons to be child advocates. It is not a theoretical discussion of child advocacy as an academic concept. I have written it for the hundreds of thousands of parents and staff persons who care about children and want to know how to help children get what they deserve.

My own experiences as a parent and staff person are the basis for the concepts and examples used. This material has been shaped by questions asked and experiences shared with students in the child advocacy course I teach at Temple University, and by my own experience as a parent active in advocacy groups.

This book is intended to stimulate the thinking and action of persons who are working on behalf of children. Child advocacy is a concept that gives greater meaning and clarity to the work that many people have been doing. Reading about and reflecting upon the role of the child advocate will focus and inspire more effective action on behalf of children. Margaret Mead has asserted:

> Only by involving adults, all adults—adults who have never had children and adults whose children have grown up—can we hope to combine reform in the care of specific groups of children—deaf children, crippled children, orphaned children—with a genuine attempt to rethink the way our towns and cities are built and the way our lives are lived. . . .[2]

The goal is to involve more adults and young people as child advocates, who will join together to demand nationwide quality children's services while continuing their local efforts to guarantee that all America's children enjoy the services and rights they deserve.

As you read, reflect on how to be more effective as a child advocate, how to sensitize and involve more adults and young people as advocates and, yes, even begin to envision a nationwide child advocacy network and system that will insure basic care, love and opportunity for every child.

Notes

1. See *America's Children 1976,* National Council of Organizations for Children and Youth, 1910 K St., N.W., Room 404, Washington, D.C., 20006, for usefully illustrated facts. Contact them or the Children's Defense Fund, 1520 New Hampshire Ave., N.W., Washington, D.C., 20036 for current statistics.

2. *Journal of Current Social Issues,* 1975.

CHAPTER ONE

SOME DEFINITIONS AND BACKGROUND

"Child advocate" sounds important, but what does it mean? Many people know what a child advocate is but have difficulty defining the term. Let's look at some definitions of *child advocate* in the context of some actual cases that illustrate its meaning.

The Child Advocate Acts on Behalf of Children

A child advocate is an actor on behalf of children. In that role, he/she is a defender, protector, mediator, supporter, investigator, negotiator, monitor, promoter, enabler, and/or counselor for children. Notice that these are all action words.

The story of Barbara Greenwald of Kalamazoo, Michigan, who acts as an advocate for a twelve-year-old boy, John Leslie, illustrates the roles of mediator, supporter, and enabler.

John had been institutionalized and diagnosed as paraplegic and mentally retarded with cerebral palsy. Through Barbara's and John's teachers' efforts, however, he has been re-evaluated and now classified mainly as physically impaired. It is hoped that in the near future he will be placed in a small barrier-free foster home when one becomes available.

John is nonverbal. His original diagnosis probably came about because he cannot express himself.

13

Barbara, who is a consultant for Family and Children's Services of Kalamazoo, has been John's advocate for two years. He enjoys sporting events, so she has taken him to hockey and football games. She also takes him to the movies, and they even go shopping although he is in a wheelchair.

She can tell when he enjoys something they do because of the way he beams. When he doesn't, he sticks out his tongue. She occasionally lets him stay at her home to broaden his adaptability to life outside the institution. Barbara believes his institutional confinement made it difficult for him to show any emotion. Others who have watched his progress, however, say that since he has had an advocate he has begun to open up more and demonstrate his feelings.

John has been learning Bliss symbols as a means of communication. This is particularly effective for people with cerebral palsy. Words are combined with symbols on his wheelchair. Now he can use his Bliss symbols to communicate to other people.

One day when John was having a meal at Barbara's house, he pointed for the first time to the Bliss symbols so that they spelled, "I love you." Barbara says she nearly cried.

She was instrumental in changing his educational program. She even goes out of her way to get his hair cut by a personal barber, not the one who clips the hair of the other 100 residents of John's facility.

Asked about her feelings towards John, she answered, "I have made a good friend."[1]

The Child Advocate Moves Bureaucracies

Effective action on behalf of children usually requires moving bureaucracies. Seeing that institutions are more responsive to the needs of the children that they were set up to serve is a major function of child advocates in our complex, bureaucratic society.

Child advocates can take a two-pronged approach: to obtain more responsive, adequate and effective services for children and families, and to develop the strengths, initiatives, and skills of those families so they can solve their own problems and be their own advocates.

The definition of a child advocate as a person who moves bureaucracies is illustrated by this story of Mark. Actually, a number of child advocates coordinated their skills and resources to help. Mark is an eleven-year-old boy whose mother's whereabouts are unknown. He sees his father only sporadically. In spring 1975, Mark became a problem in his classroom and was evaluated to determine whether he was a deprived child and therefore entitled to the services of the Philadelphia Department of Public Welfare. Instead, he was evaluated as mentally retarded and committed to Woodhaven Center, an affiliate of Temple University. There he was entitled to state mental health and mental retardation services.

At Woodhaven, Mark received a comprehensive program designed specifically for him and implemented by staff members who cared. After three months, Mark was reevaluated and judged to be normal, although his emotional problems were creating a learning disability. The Woodhaven staff determined that Mark should leave Woodhaven to be placed in a foster home and that he no longer be labelled mentally retarded. At this point, the mental health and mental retardation Base Service Unit, which tries to ensure continuity when a person is ready to return to the community (through locating community placement and providing needed counseling and evaluations), refused to provide services for Mark because he had demonstrated that he was not mentally retarded. They referred Mark to the Department of Public Welfare, Child Services Division. This office then responded that no services were available.

Temple/Woodhaven's attorney, Thomas Coval, was instructed to rejoin that this position was not acceptable and to begin legal proceedings so that the court could determine which agency would pay for Mark's placement in the community. The Court of Common Pleas ordered the Philadelphia Department of Public Welfare to find a foster home and ordered the School District of Philadelphia to plan an educational public school program within ninety days. Meanwhile, the Temple/Woodhaven staff were instructed to begin a search for Mark's foster parents.

Four months later, the Temple/Woodhaven attorneys, the Philadelphia Department of Public Welfare (Child Services), the Base Service Unit, a child advocate, and Mark returned to the chambers of Judge Frank J. Montemuro, administrative judge of the Court of Common Pleas, Philadelphia County Family Division. At this hearing, the Department of Public Welfare stated that it was still unable to find a community foster home for Mark. Woodhaven advised the court that it was prepared to identify appropriate foster parents, train them to deal with Mark's needs, and provide assistance and support as well as develop an educational public school program for Mark. The Temple/Woodhaven staff offered to implement the plan and asked the court to order the cost to be paid by the Philadelphia Department of Public Welfare.

After hearing the arguments, Judge Montemuro ordered that Mark be placed in the foster home located by the university's staff, that the Base Service Unit provide follow-along community services, and that the Philadelphia Department of Public Welfare pay the costs.

Coval views the significance of the judge's ruling as having a profound impact on the funding processes for human services in Pennsylvania "because it made all agencies responsible for the good and welfare of an eleven-year-old."[2]

Moving bureaucracies to get services that Mark needed required cooperative efforts by several assertive child advocates.

The Child Advocate Changes Systems

The child advocate aims to change systems rather than focus on individual case problems. While individual case or group situations may be the focal point to generate systems change, the advocate does not just apply Band Aids to an endless stream of cases. The advocate searches for ways to solve the problems of an entire class of cases through systems change. The goal is to alter the systems to make permanent changes that will benefit all future children who use the system.

Most child advocates begin with a specific child needing help. This is called "case advocacy." One may begin by moving a bureaucracy to secure a needed service for that child. But the advocate does not stop there. He/she takes the next steps and moves to "class advocacy." He/she may negotiate a policy or procedural change to make the services more accessible to other children, may lobby to get the service expanded or modified, or may take legal action to improve the scope, quality, or delivery of the service.

Patrick T. Murphy, who headed the Chicago Juvenile Aid Society, is a passionate advocate of basic change in the juvenile justice system. In *Our Kindly Parent . . . The State* he describes how he used case advocacy to move bureaucracies on behalf of classes of mistreated children. Assessing his work he concluded that basic change in systems are needed.

> After we took over the running of the Juvenile Legal Aid Society, we turned away many requests for legal representation that previously would have been taken. Since we referred these

cases to the public defender, the children did not go without legal representation. But we received a great deal of criticism from judges and other lawyers for cutting our case load, and much of it was well deserved. On many occasions, we turned away from our office extremely needy and deserving clients, and I am certain that as a result some families were separated which should never have been and that some children who were either innocent or had committed insignificant offenses were sent to prison. In general, the cutting of our case load probably made for a small increase in the suffering endured by the thousands of people whose "best interests" are served by the juvenile bureaucracies. But the choice was between continuing to represent hundreds of individual clients over the years, doing a marginally somewhat better job at it than the public defender's office, or concentrating on a few cases, doing them as well as we possibly could, and trying to bring about changes that might make the system better for those people unfortunate enough to have to go through it. As it was, we seldom worked less than a twelve-hour day and normally worked part of each day over weekends.

Of course, we could have kept the same long hours representing many hundreds of individual clients in the Juvenile Court, but it is simply impossible to do such a large volume of courtroom representation *and* meaningful appellate work at the same time. We did represent clients in the Juvenile Court, but we gradually cut our case load from approximately twenty-five cases a day between the two of us to perhaps twelve cases a week between the three of us. The rest of the time we worked on federal and appellate cases and, later, spent long hours on investigation of Illinois' three child-saving agencies. Although we did cut our case load we did not concentrate on what are sometimes called law-reform cases—taking one or two cases and hoping for a big appellate decision that will serve as a precedent. I felt that too often these cases did little to reform bureaucracies but served mainly as ego-boosting devices for lawyers. We termed our practice Alinsky law—using a variety of legal actions (some valid, some spurious), investigations, and intelligent use of the media to try to move, embarrass, and change bureaucracies.

During our first weeks on the job, Chris, Lew, and I outlined areas which we felt required immediate attention, and began to litigate in them. Among problems we focused on were : 1) the incarceration of children for running away from home; 2) the separating of children from poor parents on "neglect" charges, when, in fact, the parents were merely indigent and not really neglectful; and 3) certain procedural defects in the court system, such as the refusal of the Court to inform parents and children of the consequences of an "admission" of guilt, and refusal of the public defender's office to appeal cases.

After three years of trying to reform the bureaucracies of Illinois' juvenile justice system, we could look back with some justifiable pride on our accomplishments. When we began, Sheridan had well over 300 juvenile inmates, but three years and four lawsuits later, there were none. Three years previously, the Audy Home had almost 400 minors, of whom about a third were "neglected," but by 1973 there were only about 200 children in the Audy Home, of whom less than twenty-five were wards of the DCFS. The incarceration of runaways had increased tremendously over the three years, and in 1972 the Illinois legislature enacted a law that outlawed it entirely by July 1973. The number of children not in need of mental-health care, but placed in mental homes nevertheless, was rapidly diminishing. New regulations we had forced on the DMH through our litigation greatly limited the use of punishments, drugs, and the institutionalization of youthful inmates in maximum security jails. Moreover, the children under eighteen now had a right to a hearing. . . .

Still, when we detached ourselves and tried for that objectivity which allows one to see the forest instead of the trees, we had the kind of desperate feeling that Canute may have had when he tried to order the sea to recede. There had been change and movement; our lawsuits helped to expose areas of abuse and lent credence to a popular academic point of view that the problem with the juvenile-justice system is not that it has been tried and found wanting but that it has never been tried; we were often congratulated on our lawsuits by professionals for exposing the portions of the juvenile justice system which needed reform. To a certain degree, we did make an unequal, outmoded, never-really-functioning system operate more smoothly, and, hence, we not only prolonged it but gave it the aura of workability.

Those most intimately involved with juvenile and child

welfare systems over the past decades have argued that all that was needed to make the system work was more money. But our feeling—even after all these successful lawsuits—was that we could pour the same amount of money into this system that we now pour into defense and still have little to show for it as long as the system remained the same. A judicial system, juvenile, criminal, or civil, is meant to resolve disputes between claimants which cannot be resolved out of court, and to punish those individuals who somehow upset society's balance. Trying to make a court become a rehabilitative social instrument has been a noble experiment, but nevertheless a failure.[3]

Case/Class Advocacy

The process of moving from case advocacy to class advocacy has been part of the experience that has shaped and informed this book. In retrospect, I began with "case advocacy"—working to find a good school experience for my own three children. Fortunately, the neighborhood in which we were living had a strong tradition of groups working together to secure community services. In 1969 my oldest son, John, enrolled in the Powelton Mantua Parent Cooperative Nursery, one of fourteen in the city. The teacher and supplies were funded by the School District of Philadelphia and the community provided the facility which, in this case, was two ill-equipped rooms in a boys' and girls' club. The facility was used by many groups and was very poorly designed for small children. In addition, other parents in the group were finding that the positive, eager attitude toward school and learning that their children had had in nursery school was being stifled or destroyed when they entered the first grade in a formal classroom. The parent group decided to raise money from private foundations and businesses to buy and rehabilitate several vacant row houses in order to create a new school. The Children's School, as it was named, opened in the fall of 1971. It serves children ages three to eight. The parent group had to do some persistent lobbying with central school administration to get the Children's School properly funded as part of the public school system. The Children's School building is owned by the Fund, a community organization. The School District of Philadelphia rents space and operates the school.

So our individual cases were joined together into a class action to develop a new school to meet the needs of children in the neighborhood. The same group of parents formed an ongoing community organization, the Powelton Mantua Educational Fund, and worked to secure both open classrooms and traditional classrooms at each grade level in the local elementary school. The Fund has also helped establish a public school for the middle years, has developed a reading program in cooperation with five neighborhood schools and runs a summer reading and arts program.

My experience with case advocacy moving into class advocacy was part of the background I brought to forming a city-wide independent parents' organization—Parents' Union for Public Schools in Philadelphia. Arising out of the crisis created by a twelve-week teacher's strike in 1972-73, Parents' Union was formed to be the voice and bargaining agent for parents. They clearly saw that the needs of the children were

not being represented by the teachers' union or by the school board, which was acting as the agent of the political power structure of the city.

Parents' Union developed primarily to focus on system-wide policies and issues that cannot be solved at the local school or neighborhood level. However, Parents' Union has a Parent Advocate Service that does case advocacy for individual students and parents having difficulties. A Parents' Union Advocate assigned to each case assists the parent with information on rights or policies and provides assistance in resolving problems with school officials.

Case advocacy is then used as the basis for identifying and documenting the places in the system where children are being poorly served. The cases are used to press for changes in policies and procedures in the whole system.

Two Cases in Special Education Illustrating Malfunctions in the System and Parents' Union Change Procedures

1) Parents' Union was contacted by the mother of Lisa M. Lisa is thirteen years old and is classified as learning disabled. The school system placed her in a high school with 50 percent of her program in the Resource Room to remediate her reading and math deficits. Lisa was to go to regular classrooms for American history and biology, both of which are required for graduation from high school.

Because Lisa's reading deficit was so severe, she could not handle the reading requirements of those courses. Lisa does, however, have an I.Q. indicating the ability to graduate with a full diploma. Lisa's mother wished her to graduate with a full diploma.

The supervisor of the Resource Rooms in Philadelphia was contacted and attended a meeting at which he agreed to work with the Resource Room teacher and adjust the material in American history and biology to Lisa's level.

Parents' Union's Special Education Committee, in its monthly meetings with the executive director of Special Education, brought up the question: Is curriculum being planned for secondary school minimally handicapped students to ensure their graduation with a full diploma? The school system formed a curriculum committee; this committee formulated different curricula for all handicapped conditions both at the elementary and secondary levels. Pilot programs using these adjusted curricula should begin in January 1980. Parents' Union support on behalf of one child and subsequent intervention at a city-wide level resulted in a policy change affecting hundreds of students (all Special Education students) in the school system.

2) Timothy is ten years old and a bright boy. He spent his early years in school at a public school center for the learning disabled. He was sent to his neighborhood school to a regular classroom and a Resource Room program of one period per day. In January of 1979, his first year in this program, Timothy's mother called Parents' Union. Timothy was making no progress educationally, and his emotional state had regressed considerably. He was crying a lot and being harassed and intimidated by his peers in the regular classroom. There had been no contact—except for sending records—between the sending school and the receiving school. No support system had been set up to insure Timothy's successful mainstreaming. There had been no evaluative process to determine whether Timothy was emotionally ready for a regular classroom.

After a psychiatric evaluation was done, meetings were held with Timothy's teachers, counselor, mother, and a therapist from Family Services who was seeing Timothy and his family. A support and monitoring program was devised to help Timothy adjust to a regular school program and to his peers.

The question of support and monitoring for children coming out of self-contained classes was discussed with the executive director of Special Education by Parents' Union's Special Education Committee. As a result, a committee concerning "least restrictive environment" has been convened by the school system to develop policy and procedures on mainstreaming. Clarifying the school system's responsibility regarding mainstreaming will benefit a great many exceptional children.[4]

The Child Advocate Is Not

The definitions given so far may seem very broad. So let's look briefly at what a child advocate is *not*. He/she is not any and everyone working with children or in children's services. He/she is not necessarily the person providing direct services. Rather, the child advocate is the person acting on behalf of children to see that institutions and systems serve children's interests.

A person's primary role may be as a parent, nurse, teacher, social worker, or child-care worker. The person functions in that primary role most of the time, but steps into the role of child advocate when specific action for the best interest of children is needed. For example, the child-care worker may spend 95 percent of the workweek interacting with the children and other staff members and carrying out the assigned responsibilities of the job. Yet the child-care worker may observe that the treatment plan for one particular child needs modification sooner than expected, and arrange to have it brought up for a case conference. Thus, the child-care worker shifts into the role of child advocate to see that the institution responds to the child's needs and guarantees the child's rights to proper treatment.

The child advocate is *not* necessarily the same as the parent's advocate, the staff person's advocate, or the institution's advocate. The interests and rights of children are at times in conflict with the interests and rights of parents, staff persons, or other power groups in a system.

As the adjoining cartoon aptly illustrates, parents may form

organizations and engage in intense activity to preserve their right as parents to send their child to the neighborhood school. This may not be what the child needs or wants.

The child advocate is *not* a "child saver." The paternalistic assumptions that pervade the child saver's approach too often create a dependency relationship that undermines the goal of equipping the child or the child's parent to negotiate the system and to be his/her own advocate. The child saving mentality can inhibit the person from making systems changes that would enable the child or the child's parent to be listened to and respected as a person with rights.[5]

The well-intentioned "child savers" often do something *for* the child rather than *on behalf of* the child. Too often the "child savers" are certain that they are acting in the child's best interests rather than struggling to ascertain the child's best interests by weighing the complexities and by listening intently to the child's feelings and opinions.

Child saving with its overtones of paternalism permeated the thinking of the leaders who established the juvenile court system.[6] Instead of locating the cause of delinquent behavior in the economic system that spawned unemployment and poverty, the architects of the juvenile justice system advocated "reforming" the child in a residential setting away from the child's "deprived" home and "crime-infested" neighborhood. The decision about the child's future was placed in the hands of the "benevolent" judge who was supposed to act in the child's best interest. As Justice Abe Fortas acknowledged in the 1967 *Gault* decision that set due process limits on the arbitrary action of juvenile court judges:

> The early conception of the Juvenile Court proceeding was one in which a fatherly judge touched heart and conscience of the erring youth by talking over his problems, by paternal advice and admonition, and in which, in extreme situations, benevolent and wise institutions of the State provided guidance and help.[7]

Good intentions do not automatically lead to action that is in the best interest of the child.

The child advocate or even an advocacy system is *not* a substitute for a decent family social policy. Family-centered health, housing, employment, recreation, education, and child-care systems are all part of that comprehensive social policy. The advocate may work to establish those systems and policies, but does not directly provide those services. The advocate sees that the checks and balances in the system work to protect the child's interests and sees that the bureaucracies resist their inherent tendency to be self-serving.

The Focus of Advocates

Child advocates focus their action on the parts of the system or specific institution that need to be changed in order to meet the needs of children. As outlined in the national child advocacy study by the Department of Health, Education, and Welfare,[8] the action may focus on any of the following:

1. *Policy.* When the advocate's focus is the broad category of policy, he/she attempts to change the character of a

program, the rules of the game, eligibility requirements, and the like. For example, what is the day-care fee scale? . . . Will the welfare department pay a special clothing allowance at Easter time? Will a foster parent be permitted to adopt a child in her care?

2. *Administrative procedures.* Here, the overall policy is not in dispute, but the means of implementing it may be. For instance, must the mother ask for the clothing grant in person or is a phone call adequate? . . . Are boys in the training school to be allowed home visits without notice to the parents as to when? . . . Will there be evening clinic hours so that working people do not lose pay when they need treatment?

3. *Specific personnel.* Occasionally the advocate focuses on alleged malfeasance or nonfeasance on the part of a school principal, teacher, case worker, aide, inspector, and the like. In other words, the advocate's goal is to effect a personnel change or correct someone's performance.

4. *Budgets.* The advocate may focus on assuring adequate appropriations. On the federal level, Congress votes an

authorization limit when it enacts a program, but the specific appropriation must be voted on subsequently. Some groups—e.g., lobbyists or special interests groups of parents—may concentrate on the appropriation process. . . .

5. *Laws.* If the need is for a new program, major changes in an existing program, or elimination of an existing policy, the target may be the statutory provision. Advocates often lobby for or against legislation. Sometimes they fight proposed legislation, which is turned over to members of the executive or legislative branch for formal introduction. At times the issue is fought in the courts: e.g., a client's case is the vehicle for a "class action"—a legal challenge that, if sustained, invalidates a law or leads to major new administrative departures.

6. *Political action.* A number of political organizing ventures . . . focus on children's issues and now view themselves as part of the child advocacy movement. These groups generally have the redistribution of power and resources as their ultimate goal, unlike the majority of child advocacy programs, which are concerned only with changing service systems.

A seventh area of focus should be added that the H.E.W. study did not include:

7. *Physical facilities.* The physical layout and condition of the school, detention center, hospital, home, clinic, playground, or residential unit may be the initial or primary focus for action by advocates. Other advocate groups may focus their attention on the wider physical environment like the traffic patterns in a neighborhood, planning of apartment complexes and shopping centers, or pollution of rivers or air.

With these definitions of the child advocate, let's look at the ways that children's rights now provide a new basis for action by the child advocate.

Notes

1. *Mental Retardation News,* March/April 1978, p. 3.
2. *The Woodhaven Staffer,* January/February 1977, vol. 4, no.1, Temple University, Commonwealth of Pennsylvania, Phila., Pa.
3. Patrick T. Murphy, *Our Kindly Parent . . . The State,* Penguin, 1977, pp. 13, 14, 169-67.
4. Parents' Union for Public Schools, 401 N. Broad St., Phila., Pa., 19108. The names of the students have been changed to protect their identities.
5. See chapter Two for further discussion.
6. See Willard Gaylin, Ira Glasser, Steven Marcus, and David Rothman, *Doing Good: The Limits of Benevolence* (New York: Pantheon Books, 1978) and Anthony Platt, *The Child Savers: The Invention of Delinquency,* 2d ed. (Chicago: The University of Chicago Press, 1977).
7. *In re Gault,* 387 U.S. 1 (1967).
8. Alfred Kahn et al., *Child Advocacy: A National Baseline Study,* H.E.W., 1972, pp. 76-77.

CHAPTER TWO

CHILDREN'S RIGHTS:
THE BASIS
FOR ADVOCACY

Children's rights are the basis for action by the child advocate. When a right exists, the child advocate no longer has to beg for a service or fair treatment. The child advocate can *assert* that child's right.

The dramatic change that occurs when a right exists as a basis for the advocate's work is illustrated by the story of the right to education for handicapped children in Pennsylvania. Prior to 1972, many parents and agency personnel had to search for private school and institutional placements for retarded children because many public schools turned these children away, claiming that they were too difficult to serve. The responsibility was left to the parents to make their own private arrangements—oftentimes caring for them at home or placing them in institutions. As the result of a lawsuit by a group of parents *(The Pennsylvania Association for Retarded Children (PARC)* v. *Commonwealth of Pennsylvania),* the court ordered in 1972 that the public schools have a legal obligation to educate retarded children. In addition, the court ordered that school districts must actively search out retarded children who have been closeted away.

That court decision had a revolutionary effect on the children, their parents and the staff in child-care agencies.

After the court had established the legal right of retarded children to a public education, parents and staff could then focus their energies on seeing that the law was implemented and that the public school system was serving the needs of retarded children rather than spending their time and resources finding private accommodations for each child. Parents did not have to beg the school district to accept their child, but could assert their child's right to a public education.

Child advocates can work in four ways to affect rights. They can:

1. establish rights through court decisions or legislation;
2. guarantee the implementation of rights;
3. monitor systems to insure that the intent of the law is enforced; and,
4. assist individual children and families to exercise their rights by providing advocacy service and by educating youth, parents and staff people.

Establishing Rights Via Court Cases and Legislation

The two major ways that rights get established are by court rulings on specific cases and by legislation passed at the federal, state or local level.

The famous case of Gerald Gault illustrates the kind of time, persistence and skill that his parents and attorney had as his advocates. The Supreme Court ruling in 1967 established that children are persons under the law and must have a lawyer and other due process safeguards in juvenile court.

The Case of Gerald Gault

The U.S. Supreme Court established due process rights for young people in juvenile court. [*In re Gault,* 387 U.S. 1 (1967)] Parts of that important decision are directly quoted below.

Basic Facts of the Case

On Monday, June 8, 1964, at about 10 A.M., Gerald Francis Gault and a friend, Ronald Lewis, were taken into custody by the Sheriff of Gila County. Gerald was then still subject to a six months' probation order which had been entered on February 25, 1964, as a result of his having been in the company of another boy who had stolen a wallet from a lady's purse. The police action on June 8 was taken as the result of a verbal complaint by a neighbor of the boys, Mrs. Cook, about a telephone call made to her in which the caller or callers made lewd or indecent remarks. It will suffice for purposes of this opinion to say that the remarks or questions put to her were of the irritatingly offensive, adolescent, sex variety.

At the time Gerald was picked up, his mother and father were both at work. No notice that Gerald was being taken into custody was left at the home. No other steps were taken to advise them that their son had, in effect, been arrested. Gerald was taken to the Children's Detention Home. When his mother arrived home at about 6 o'clock, Gerald was not there. Gerald's older brother was sent to look for him at the trailer home of the Lewis family. He apparently learned then that Gerald was in custody. He so informed his mother. The two of them went to the Detention Home. The deputy probation officer, Flagg, who was also superintendent of the Detention Home, told Mrs. Gault "why Jerry was there" and said that a hearing would be held in Juvenile Court at 3 o'clock the following day, June 9.

Officer Flagg filed a petition with the court on the hearing day, June 9, 1964. It was not served on the Gaults. Indeed, none of them saw this petition until the habeas corpus hearing on August 17, 1964. The petition was entirely formal. It made no reference to any factual basis for the judicial action which it initiated. It recited only that "said minor is under the age of eighteen years, and is in need of the protection of this Honorable Court; [and that] said minor is a delinquent." It prayed for a hearing and an order regarding "the care and custody of said minor." Officer Flagg executed a formal affidavit in support of the petition.

On June 9, Gerald, his mother, his older brother, and Probation Officers Flagg and Henderson appeared before the Juvenile Judge in chambers. Gerald's father was not there. He was at work out of the city. Mrs. Cook, the complainant, was not there. No one was sworn in at this hearing. No transcript or recording was made. No memorandum or record of the substance of the proceedings was prepared. Our information about the proceedings and the subsequent hearing on June 15, derives entirely from the testimony of the Juvenile Court Judge, Mr. and Mrs. Gault and Officer Flagg at the habeas corpus proceeding conducted two months later. From this, it appears that at the June 9 hearing Gerald was questioned by the judge about the telephone call. There was conflict as to what he said. His mother recalled that Gerald said he only dialed Mrs. Cook's number and handed the telephone to his friend, Ronald. Officer Flagg recalled that Gerald had admitted making the lewd remarks. Judge McGhee testified that Gerald "admitted making one of these [lewd] statements." At the conclusion of the hearings, the judge said he would "think about it." Gerald was taken back to the Detention Home. He was not sent to his own home with his parents. On June 11 or 12, after having been detained since June 8, Gerald was released and driven home. There is no explanation in the record as to why he was kept in the Detention Home or why he was released. At 5 P.M. on the day of Gerald's release, Mrs. Gault received a note signed by Officer Flagg. It was on plain paper, not letterhead. Its entire text was as follows:

Mrs. Gault:

Judge McGhee has set Monday, June 15, 1964 at 11:00 A.M. as the date and time for further hearings on Gerald's delinquency.
S. Flagg

His Hearing in Juvenile Court

At the appointed time on Monday, June 15, Gerald, his father and mother, Ronald Lewis and his father, and Officers Flagg and Henderson were present before Judge McGhee. Witnesses at the habeas corpus proceeding differed in their recollections of Gerald's testimony at the June 15 hearing. Mr. and Mrs. Gault recalled that Gerald again testified that he had only dialed the number and that the other boy had made the remarks. Officer Flagg agreed that at this hearing Gerald did not admit making the lewd remarks. But Judge McGhee recalled that "there was some admission again of some of the lewd statements. He didn't admit any of the more serious lewd statements." Again, the complainant, Mrs. Cook, was not present. Mrs. Gault asked that Mrs. Cook be present "so she could see which boy had done the talking, the dirty talking over the phone." The Juvenile Judge said "she didn't have to be present at that hearing." The judge did not speak to Mrs. Cook or communicate with her at any time. Probation Officer Flagg had talked to her once . . . over the telephone on June 9.

At this June 15 hearing a "referral report" made by the probation officers was filed with the court, although not disclosed to Gerald or his parents. This listed the charge as "Lewd Phone Calls." At the conclusion of the hearing, the judge committed Gerald as a juvenile delinquent to the State Industrial School " for the period of his minority [that is, until 21], unless sooner discharged by due process of law." An order to that effect was entered. It recites that "after a full hearing and due deliberation the Court finds that said minor is a delinquent child, and that said minor is of the age of fifteen years."

Appeals During the Next Two Years

No appeal is permitted by Arizona law in juvenile cases. On August 3, 1964, a petition for a writ of habeas corpus was filed with the Supreme Court of Arizona and referred by it to the Superior Court for hearing.

At the habeas corpus hearing on August 17, Judge McGhee was vigorously cross-examined as to the basis for his actions. He testified that he had taken into account the fact that Gerald was on probation. He was asked "under what section of . . . the code you found the boy delinquent?"

His answer is set forth in the margin. "Q. All right. Now, Judge, would you tell me under what section of the law or tell me under what section of—of the code you found the boy delinquent?" "A. Well, there is a—I think it amounts to disturbing the peace. I can't give you the section, but I can tell you the law, that when one person uses lewd language in the presence of another person, that it can amount to—and I consider that when a person makes it over the phone, that it is considered in the presence, I might be wrong, that is one section. The other section upon which I consider the boy delinquent is Section 8-201, Subsection (d), habitually involved in immoral matters." [Notes in original.]

In substance, he concluded that Gerald came within ARS Section 8-201-6(a), which specificies that a "delinquent child" includes one who has violated a law of the state or an ordinance or regulation of a political subdivision thereof." The law which Gerald was found to have violated is ARS Section 13-377. This section of the Arizona Criminal Code provides that a person who "in the presence or hearing of any woman or child . . . uses vulgar, abusive or obscene language, is guilty of a misdemeanor. . . ." The penalty specified in the Criminal Code, which would apply to an adult, is $5 to $50, or imprisonment for not more than two months. The judge also testified that he acted under ARS Section 8-201-6(d) which includes in the definition of a "delinquent child" one who, as the judge phrased it, is "habitually involved in immoral matters."

Asked about the basis for his conclusion that Gerald

was "habitually involved in immoral matters," the judge testified, somewhat vaguely, that two years earlier, on July 2, 1962, a "referral" was made concerning Gerald, "where the boy had stolen a baseball glove from another boy and lied to the Police Department about it." The judge said there was "no hearing," and "no accusation" relating to this incident, "because of lack of material foundation." But it seems to have remained in his mind as a relevant factor. The judge also testified that Gerald had admitted making other nuisance phone calls in the past which, as the judge recalled the boy's testimony, were "silly calls, or funny calls, or something like that."

The Superior Court dismissed the writ, and appellants sought review in the Arizona Supreme Court. That court stated that it considered appellants' assignments of error as urging (1) that the Juvenile Code, ARS Section 8-201 to Section 8-239, is unconstitutional because it does not require that parents and children be apprised of the specific charges, does not require proper notice of a hearing, and does not provide for an appeal; and (2) that the proceedings and order relating to Gerald constituted a denial of due process law because of the absence of adequate notice of the charge and the hearing; failure to notify appellants of certain constitutional rights including the rights to counsel and to confrontation, and the privilege against self-incrimination; the use of unsworn hearsay testimony; and the failure to make a record of the proceedings. Appellants further asserted that it was error for the Juvenile Court to remove Gerald from the custody of his parents without a showing and finding of their unsuitability, and alleged a miscellany of other errors under state law.

The Arizona Supreme Court handed down an elaborate and wide-ranging opinion affirming dismissal of the writ and stating the court's conclusions as to the issues raised by appellants and other aspects of the juvenile process. In their jurisdictional statement and brief in this Court, appellants do not urge upon us all of the points passed upon by the Supreme Court of Arizona. They urge that we hold the Juvenile Code of Arizona invalid on its face or as applied in this case because, contrary to the Due Process Clause of the Fourteenth Amendment, the juvenile is taken from the custody of his parents and committed to a state institution pursuant to proceedings in which the Juvenile Court has virtually unlimited discretion, and in which the following basic rights are denied:

1. notice of the charges;
2. right to counsel;
3. right to confrontation and cross-examination;
4. privilege against self-incrimination;
5. right to a transcript of the proceedings; and
6. right to appellate review.

The Supreme Court's Decision—May 15, 1967

Ultimately, however, we confront the reality of that portion of the Juvenile Court process with which we deal in this case. A boy is charged with misconduct. The boy is committed to an institution where he may be restrained of liberty for years. It is of no constitutional consequence—and of limited practical meaning—that the institution to which he is committed is called an Industrial School. The fact of the matter is that, however euphemistic the title, a "receiving home" or an "industrial school" for juveniles is an institution of confinement in which the child is incarcerated for a greater or lesser time. . . . Instead of mother and father and sisters and brothers and friends and classmates, his world is peopled by guards, custodians, state employees, and "delinquents" confined with him for anything from waywardness to rape and homicide.

In view of this, it would be extraordinary if our Constitution did not require the procedural regularity and the exercise of care implied in the phrase "due process." Under our Constitution, the condition of being

a boy does not justify *a kangaroo court*. The traditional
ideas of Juvenile Court procedure, indeed, contemplated
that time would be available and care would be used to
establish precisely what the juvenile did and why he did
it—was it a prank of adolescence or a brutal act
threatening serious consequences to himself or society
unless corrected? Under traditional notions, one would
assume that in a case like that of Gerald Gault, where the
juvenile appears to have a home, a working mother and
father, and an older brother, the Juvenile Judge would
have made a careful inquiry and judgment as to the
possibility that the boy could be disciplined and dealt with
at home, despite his previous transgressions. Indeed, so
far as appears in the record before us, except for some
conversation with Gerald about his school work and his
"wanting to go to . . . The Grand Canyon with his father,"
the points to which the judge directed his attention were
little different from those that would be involved in
determining any charge of violation of a penal statute.
The essential difference between Gerald's case and a
normal criminal case is that safeguards available to adults
were discarded in Gerald's case. The summary procedure as well as the long commitment was possible because
Gerald was fifteen years of age instead of over eighteen.

If Gerald had been over eighteen, he would not have
been subject to Juvenile Court proceedings. For the
particular offense immediately involved, the maximum
punishment would have been a fine of $5 to $50, or
imprisonment in jail for not more than two months.
Instead, he was committed to custody for a maximum of
six years. If he had been over eighteen and had
committed an offense to which such a sentence might
apply, he would have been entitled to substantial rights
under the Constitution of the United States as well as
under Arizona's laws and constitution. . . .

Where a person, infant or adult, can be seized by the
State, charged, and convicted for violating a state
criminal law, and then ordered by the State to be

confined for six years, I think the Constitution requires that he be tried in accordance with the guarantees of all the provisions of the Bill of Rights made applicable to the States by the Fourteenth Amendment. Undoubtedly this would be true of an adult defendant, and it would be a plain denial of equal protection of the laws—an invidious discrimination—to hold that others subject to heavier punishments could, because they are children, be denied these same constitutional safeguards. I consequently agree with the Court that the Arizona law as applied here denied to the parents and their son the right of notice, right to counsel, right against self-incrimination, and right to confront the witness against young Gault. Appellants are entitled to these rights, not because "fairness, impartiality and orderliness—in short, the essentials of due process"—require them and not because they are "the procedural rules which have been fashioned from the generality of due process," but because they are specifically and unequivocally granted by provisions of the Fifth and Sixth Amendments which the Fourteenth Amendment makes applicable to the States.

Gerald Gault's family and attorneys worked three years to free Gerald and to secure these rights for all young people. (Countless other young people have spent years in state training schools or reformatories.) Gault's cause came to light because of persistent advocacy by his parents. Juvenile court Judge McGhee committed Gerald Gault, age fifteen, as a juvenile delinquent to the State Industrial School for a period of his minority (that is, until twenty-one) unless sooner discharged by due process of law. Gerald's alleged crime was making lewd telephone calls.

Mrs. Marjorie Gault had gone to that juvenile court hearing without a lawyer and was expecting Gerald to be released after being "taught a good lesson." He had been kept at a Detention Home from the day he was picked up, Monday, June 8, 1964, until the hearing on Monday, June 15.

Mrs. Gault was stunned by the severity of the sentence. Mrs.

Gault told Judge McGhee that she would get a lawyer, but was then told that no appeal of juvenile cases was permitted by Arizona law. Mr. and Mrs. Gault did contact an attorney, Amelie D. Lewis, who advised them that they could at least try to file a writ of habaeus corpus, arguing that Gerald's commitment to the state training school was illegal because he had not had a real hearing with a lawyer present to argue his case and cross-examine witnesses. On August 3, 1964, they filed in the supreme court of Arizona, which referred the case to the Superior Court. The Superior Court turned down their argument, so they appealed it to the Arizona Supreme Court. Again they lost.

Mr. and Mrs. Gault and their attorney persisted—and secured the assistance of two nationally known lawyers of the American Civil Liberties Union—Norman Dorson and Melvin L. Wulf. After two more years of legal preparation and maneuvering, the Supreme Court ruled in Gerald Gault's favor on May 15, 1967.

Rights Established by Legislation

Children's rights are also established by legislation. Child abuse laws have been passed in many state legislatures, making child abusers subject to criminal penalties and requiring that suspected child abuse be reported to the authorities by doctors, nurses, teachers, child-care workers, counselors and neighbors.

The Education for All Handicapped Children Act, passed by the U. S. Congress in 1975, very clearly spells out the right of all children to an education and details the rights of handicapped children and their parents to be involved in decisions about the placement and educational plan. This federal legislation was the result of years of work by many advocates and advocacy organizations. As early as 1898, Alexander Graham Bell had publicly advocated the right to an education in public schools for handicapped children, even though the courts had made rulings denying public education to "feebleminded" children (1893). The parents and lawyers in the PARC case of 1972 got that earlier decision overturned. Advocates in other states initiated test cases in their state courts. In addition, coalitions of parents, lawyers and politicians secured the passage of legislation at the state level that paved the way for federal legislation. Advocacy organizations like the Council for Exceptional Children prepared model legislation that was used by political leaders in Congress. Advocacy organizations also lobbied and testified at hearings, heightening the awareness of the public and their congressional representatives. The Education Commission of the States and the Bureau of the Education for the Handicapped (HEW) also used their skill and clout. The vote of 404 to 7 in the House of Representatives and 87 to 7 in the Senate was the result of all these advocates joining forces to establish this federal law.

Implementing Rights

Court cases are won in court, and legislation gets written by lawmakers. But many times the advocates' role is just beginning. Translating the *words* in the court order or legislation into *programs and procedures* in the school system, juvenile justice system, and health care systems, which provide safeguards and services for children, is the next task. The journey from the courtroom to the classroom, or from the legislature to the police station is often a long and arduous one.

Using the *Gault* case as an example, Judge Lisa Richette reports in *Throw-away Children* some of the problems that she encountered. Implementing the spirit and letter of the law was difficult. She notes:

> The Supreme Court did not include in its opinion a how-to-do-it set of instructions to juvenile courts. Presumably, they will get the message without such a kit.
>
> Six months after the *Gault* decision, I represented a boy charged with a series of burglaries in an outlying suburb of Philadelphia. On the day of his hearing, several local lawyers came up to me in the courthouse corridor and, knowing that I

was a stranger, warned me that the judge had his own way of doing things, the *Gault* decision notwithstanding.

"Above all," they advised, "don't be too legalistic. He doesn't like lawyers to argue too hard."

Armed with this good advice, I walked into the hearing room. The detectives who had arrested the boy prepared themselves to testify. We all waited for ten minutes while the boy's probation officer, seated next to the judge, spoke to him in a low voice. I could not make out his words, but observing the judge's head-nodding, his thumbing of a mass of reports, and his occasional glances in our direction, I knew they were discussing the boy.

Knowing that to protest at this point would start me off on *two* wrong feet, I nevertheless stood up to object.

The judge told me to sit down. I held my ground and explained that the court was receiving possibly prejudicial information which I could neither challenge by cross-examination nor answer in rebuttal.

"Don't worry," said the judge, "I always keep an open mind. Just remember, young lady, that you're going to have a hard time convincing me that I shouldn't send him away for at least a year." (After several other "hearings" in which the judge remained adamant, he ordered the boy off to a training school.)[1]

In addition to the problem of judges who resisted the intent of the *Gault* decision, finding lawyers to represent adequately the many children who needed court-appointed attorneys because their families were nonexistent or could not afford to pay private attorneys' fees was another major problem. Judge Richette described the confusion, case overloads and roadblocks she witnessed in just one city. The Voluntary Defender Association was set up by the Philadelphia Bar Association and then Community Legal Services lawyers were assigned cases by the judges. She notes:

It was an impossible mission, doomed from the onset. Neither four nor even forty lawyers could represent even a significant percentage of the children needing counsel. While they waited for lawyers to interview them, or their cases to be listed for hearing, children remained in detention. In December 1967, the Community Legal Services lawyers closed their doors to any more court-appointed juvenile clients. Shortly afterward, the head of that group resigned.

The situation was described in the Philadelphia *Evening Bulletin* as one of "turmoil at the County Court." Between February 4 and March 24 of 1968, four able judges tendered their resignations from duty in the Juvenile Division because they could no longer endure the daily frustrations in court.[2]

Implementing the Education for All Handicapped Children Act (P.L. 94-142) is also a tedious and ongoing process. The law passed Congress in 1975, and school districts were given until September 1978 to prepare the system for identifying, testing and placing, and educating eligible children. During the 1978-79 school year, many districts experienced a lack of qualified personnel to do testing; principals, teachers and counselors who had relatively little knowledge or experience with handicapped children; a shortage of properly trained special education teachers; lack of supplies and properly equipped classrooms, bathrooms, cafeterias and gymnasiums; and a shortage of buses to transport children to the proper school. There were delays of up to a year in getting children tested and placed; in the meantime they adjusted to a series of substitutes, until properly trained special education teachers could be placed, and waited in the cold for buses that sometimes didn't come.

Five years after the passage of the law, some school districts are still doing initial testing, and are waiting for qualified teachers to staff classrooms. Attention is only beginning to be focused on sensitizing classroom teachers and students to the needs and feelings of handicapped children who are being mainstreamed or educated to the greatest degree possible with children who are not handicapped. P.L. 94-142 requires that handicapped children be placed in "special classes, separate schooling or other removal from the regular educational environment . . . only when the nature or severity of the handicap is such that education in regular classes with the use of supplementary aids and services cannot be achieved satisfactorily." Implementing this part of the law takes years of efforts by child advocates at all levels of the systems—at the federal, state and local level and at all levels of each school district.

Monitoring the Letter and Spirit of Laws

Laws don't enforce themselves; that takes people. Child advocates serve as watchdogs over systems and services to see that children get the protection and services to which they are entitled by law.

Six years after the *Gault* decision had been handed down, Judge Justice Wise Polier headed a study by the Children's Defense Fund and found the following:

> Despite this [*Gault*] ruling, there are still many courts where children and their parents are not informed of their rights. Within one state, for instance, the right to counsel varied in its implementation from 0 percent in one county to 100 percent in another. In a different state, one judge said he appointed a counsel, told him what he wanted, and if the counsel did not conform, he got other counsel. In a third state, if a counsel selected from a panel "makes waves," he finds he is not called again for a long time. In such instances, counsel rightly is seen as an agent of the court rather than as a representative of the child. Unless the counsel is independent, the right to counsel becomes a mockery.[3]

In a typical case related to the Education for All Handicapped Children Act, Mary Jones contacted an advocate service with a complaint that her ten-year-old daughter, Jennifer, was refusing to go to school. Jennifer was in a special education classroom at her neighborhood school. In the course of advising the parents how to solve her problem, the advocate showed Mrs. Jones the section in the law on her right to challenge the placement of her child and to work out an appropriate placement that meets the child's needs. After considerable fact finding, Mrs. Jones did request a hearing and a new placement for her daughter.

Some advocacy organizations are systematically monitoring the Education for All Handicapped Children Act at local and national levels. The National Committee for Citizens in Education (NCCE) urges members of its Parents' Network in local school districts to ask questions and collect data, which NCCE then assembles and presents to federal officials.

Monitoring the implementation of court orders and legislation is an ongoing process and is absolutely essential to keep any system honest.

Assisting Children and Parents to Exercise Their Rights

Unless young people and their parents know what their rights are and exercise them, their rights are worth only the paper they are printed upon. Violations occur daily; children are repeatedly denied life-giving services. But the youth or parent who knows he/she has a right to a fair procedure or service cannot be cheated so easily.

Some advocate organizations have made it their business to systematically inform young people and parents of their rights under the law. (See chapters Six and Seven for a fuller discussion and examples.)

Advocate groups and individual advocates also provide support to young people and parents who know their rights were violated and who need help. The support or advocate assistance is perhaps in the form of documentation, relevant research, contacts with sympathetic people within the system, accompanying the young person and/or parent to a meeting or hearing, or referral to legal or social agencies.

The following case illustrates how a parent advocate of Parents' Union for Public Schools in Philadelphia assisted a parent and student. The advocate also used the case to press the school system to follow the law regarding students' rights in suspensions.

The Suspension of Vera Simon—How a
Parent Advocate Helped

In February of 1977, Parents' Union received a request to assist the family of Vera Simon (pseudonym), who had been suspended because of lateness to class. In the course of resolving the case, the Parents' Union advocate accompanied the mother and daughter to six conferences between February 17 and December 5, 1977. The conferences began with the principal and vice-principal, and later included the counselor, the district superintendent and an administrative assistant. Finally the whole issue was discussed with the superintendent of schools in January of 1978. Excerpts from a letter by the Parents' Union advocate to the superintendent show how one parent on one grievance can lead to changes that benefit many students.

Dear Superintendent Marcase:

In a recent regular monthly conference with Parents' Union which included an evaluation of the document, *Discipline in the Philadelphia Public Schools*, you expressed an interest in being informed about significant violations of the guidelines contained in the Discipline document. This letter is intended to bring such a violation to your attention.

I am referring to the suspension policies currently in practice at _____ Junior/Senior High School. My awareness of the situation at _____ School developed over a several-months period last year. A summary of events during those months will bring helpful background to my present concern.

Vera Simon [her actual name has been changed], a tenth grade student last year at _____ School, was suspended on three different occasions, each time for lateness to class.

Vera Simon, Mrs. Simon and I had an initial very disappointing conference with the vice-principal and the principal of the school. We had hoped to discuss alternative ways to deal with Vera's difficulty in getting to her early morning class on time. We had also hoped to raise some questions about the broad range of offenses for which suspensions were used as disciplinary measures. We had asked that Vera's counselor and the person in charge of the Motivation Program she was in be present at the conference as well. Neither was there. The principal refused to discuss the school's suspension policies while Mrs. Simon was present. The whole tone of the conference left us feeling humiliated and angry. Both Vera and her mother were in tears when we left. . . .

When Vera was suspended a third time on March 23, 1977 (this after only *one* additional late notice since our first conference over a month before), Mrs. Simon, Vera and I arranged for a conference with Dr. Harris at the District 4 office. Again we questioned the use of suspension for such offenses as: "excessive lateness," "in hall without a pass," "did not report for detention," "student in building after dismissal—no pass," "did not return materials to parents or other school material as requested," etc.

Instead of pursuing the matter further in his office, Dr. Harris immediately set up an appointment for us with the District Superintendent. Mrs. Simon and I met with her on March 21, 1977. At that time, the District Superintendent assured us that suspension would no longer be used as a disciplinary measure for lateness and that Vera would not be suspended for lateness again. She also agreed with us that alternatives to suspension must be found, that there is need for re-education of staff and community, and that each of the schools in District 4 was to submit to her office by May or June of 1977 a discipline document for their school which would be in compliance with the discipline guidelines for the whole school district.

We were very appreciative of that kind of support from the district office (both the content and the spirit in which it was given), but we also recognized that compliance by the individual schools with a position stated by the District Superintendent would not come automatically. This fall we discovered how true that was.

This year Vera is repeating tenth grade because of last year's setbacks due to lateness, suspensions, class cuts and general disillusionment with school. Her first report card this fall, however, showed all A's, B's and C's. Mr. Matthews, the counselor, says, "Vera has made a marked improvement over her class." But once again she has been suspended, this time for *chewing gum* and "talking back" to the vice-principal who remembers her from last year. Vera feels that what the vice-principal terms "talking back" was an exercise of her right to say why she did not think she should be suspended. Again, it appears that a serious disciplinary measure was brought to bear on an *isolated, minor* violation of the rules.

What was even more distressing was the fact that, in spite of the District Superintendent's mandate to the schools last spring, very little, if anything, had changed. . . .

Because Parents' Union has already expended so much time and energy in dialogue with _____School and District 4 on these issues in the past, we think it expedient to discuss it with you now. We would request that it be placed on the agenda for our next meeting on January 11, 1978. . . .

To summarize, it is clear that _____ School (and we suspect many other schools in Philadelphia): (1) is using suspensions for a wide variety of situations where the seriousness of the misconduct does not merit putting the student out of school . . . ; (2) is not developing and implementing alternatives to suspensions . . . ; (3) perhaps most important, it appears obvious, especially in the case of Vera Simon, that the casual use of suspension affords a far greater amount of psychological damage than remedial benefit. . . .

Therefore we wish to underline that out-of-school

suspensions would be most appropriately used for misbehaviors which materially disrupt the educational process or pose a threat to the safety and welfare of others.

Sincerely,

Arbutus B. Sider, Chairperson
Grievance Committee

It was gratifying to the Simon family and to Parents' Union to receive several weeks later a letter of apology from the principal involved, apparently under pressure from his superiors. The letter stated that in the future, his school would abide by school district policies and guidelines in the area of suspensions.

In terms of the change in the student involved, Vera Simon blossomed from a weepy, withdrawn girl during the first conference to a much more self-confident, articulate student who was aware of her rights and able to state them to officials.

Advocacy is an ongoing process of establishing, implementing, and monitoring laws and programs and assisting parents and children to exercise their rights under the law. More skilled and dedicated child advocates and advocate organizations are needed to make rights a living reality in children's lives.

Given that children's rights are the basis for effective action by the child advocate:

1. What rights *do* children have?
2. What rights *should* they have?
3. Are there rights children should *not* have?

Rights Established by Law

Relatively few rights have been established by the courts and legislation, and most of these very recently. Historically, the child was viewed as the father's property or chattel—along with animals and women! The rights of the parent were supreme.

Prior to 1967, most of the legislation or court decisions directed specifically toward children were state rather than federal regulations. The juvenile court system was established by state laws in the late 1800s and early 1900s. Compulsory education laws were passed by most states in the same period, but no federal law was enacted. Child labor regulations were enacted by state legislatures from 1902-24. The federal Child Labor Amendment to the U.S. Constitution was defeated in 1924.

However, a few actions at the federal level prior to 1967 did have a powerful effect on children's lives. For example, the Thirteenth Amendment to the Constitution in 1865 abolished slavery and thus black children were no longer the legal property of slaveowners and the practice of indenturing white children was curtailed as a side effect. In 1954 the right to a desegregated public education for black children was established by the U. S. Supreme Court (*Brown* v. *Topeka Board of Education*).

A time line noting some of the children's rights established by the federal courts or by federal legislation illustrates the dramatic changes that occurred in the decade following the 1967 *Gault* decision. That ruling was a landmark because for the first time the Supreme Court asserted that the rights in the U.S. Constitution apply to *children as persons* under the law.

1967   Due process rights for juveniles in delinquency hearings include the right to a lawyer, the right to cross-examine accusers and witnesses, the right to present evidence and witnesses on one's own behalf, the right to refuse to incriminate one's self. (*In re Gault*). This was the first clear extension of the rights of the U.S. Constitution to a child. .

1968   Children born to non-married parents have the right to sue for damages for wrongful death of their parents. The Fourteenth Amendment of Constitution applies to children and provides equal protection. (*Levy* v. *Louisiana*)[4]

1969   School students have the right to freedom of expression. They can wear black armbands to express political dissent. The First Amendment rights of Constitution apply to students in school. (*Tinker* v. *Des Moines Independent Community School District*)

1970   The state must prove the young person's guilt "beyond a reasonable doubt" in all delinquency hearings. (*In re Winship*)

1971   Eighteen-year-olds have the right to vote in federal elections. Twenty-sixth Amendment to U.S. Constitution.

1973   Children born to non-married parents have the right to be supported by their parents (*Gomez* v. *Perez*) and have the right to receive public assistance. (*New Jersey Welfare Rights Organization* v. *Cahill*)

1973   Children in a state training school and other institutions cannot be subjected to cruel and unusual punishment like beating, drugging and excessive solitary confinement. (*Morales* v. *Turman*)

1974   Parents and students (when over eighteen) have a right to examine school records and are guaranteed protection of privacy of those records. (Family Educational Rights and Privacy Act—federal legislation)

1975   Juveniles may not be prosecuted or punished twice for the same offense. The Fifth Amendment of U.S. Constitution applies to juveniles. (*Breed* v. *Jones*)

1975   Children have a right to protection against physical, emotional, or sexual abuse by adults. (federal and state child abuse legislation)

1975   School students have due process rights in cases of suspension and expulsion. (*Goss* v. *Lopez*)

1975   Handicapped children have a right to education in "the least restrictive setting." Their parents have extensive due process rights. (Education for All Handicapped Children Act Public Law 94-142—federal legislation)

1976   A young woman has a right to an abortion in the first
          trimester of her pregnancy without securing paren-
          tal consent. (*Planned Parenthood of Central Missouri* v.
          Danforth)[5]

What Rights Should Children Have?

When one asks the next question, What rights should
children have? the debate gets heated. Philosophical, social,
and political issues that surface will require the serious
attention of child advocates over the next decades. A central
question is, Should adult rights be extended to children or do
children need special protection and rights under the law
because of their immaturity, vulnerability, lack of political
power, and need for a childhood?

Those who argue that adult rights must be extended to
children propose giving children the right to vote, the right to
economic independence, the right to sexual freedom, and the
right to choose their living environment.

Richard Farson, for example, in *Birthrights* proposes a
Child's Bill of Rights that includes:

> *The Right to Alternative Home Environments.* Self-determining
> children should be able to choose from among a variety of
> arrangements: residences operated by children, child exchange
> programs, twenty-four-hour child care centers, and various
> kinds of schools and employment opportunities. . . .

> *The Right to Information.* A child must have the right to all
> information ordinarily available to adults—including, and
> perhaps especially, information that makes adults uncomfort-
> able. . . .

> *The Right to Educate Oneself.* Children should be free to design
> their own education, choosing from among many options the
> kinds of learning experiences they want, including the option
> not to attend any kind of school. Compulsory education must be
> abolished because the enforced threatening quality of educa-
> tion in America has taught children to hate school, to hate the
> subject matter, and tragically, to hate themselves. . . .

The Right to Sexual Freedom. Children should have the right to conduct their sexual lives with no more restriction than adults. Sexual freedom for children must include the right to information about sex, the right to nonsexist education, and the right to all sexual activities that are legal among consenting adults. . . .

The Right to Political Power. Children should have the vote and be included in the decision-making process. Eighty million children in the United States need the right to vote because adults do not vote in their behalf. At present they are no one's constituency and legislation reflects that lack of representation. To become a constituency they must have the right to vote.

John Holt in *Escape from Childhood* also proposes extending many adult rights to children:

I urge that the law grant and guarantee to the young the freedom that it now grants to adults to make certain kinds of choices, do certain kinds of things, and accept certain kinds of responsibilities. This means in turn that the law will take action against anyone who interferes with young people's rights to do such things. Thus when the law guarantees me the right to vote, it is not saying I must vote, it is not giving me a vote. It only says that if I choose to vote, it will act against anyone who tries to prevent me. In granting me rights, the law does not say what I must or shall do. It simply says that it will not allow other people to prevent me from doing these things.[6]

Others like Marian Wright Edelman, director of the Children's Defense Fund, sharply disagree with Holt:

In my view, much of the children's-liberation talk is just hogwash. There are some instances in which children should have adult's rights, and we have to determine which instances those are, and which children need them. But children are not adults. They need protection and nurturing. We have to analyze, case by case, what is best for children. I don't think Holt and the other liberationists have thought through the complexities of children and their needs. I'm a parent and know darned well that my five-year-old should not be liberated, and that my four-year-old is not capable of managing his money. The institutional disregard of children is pervasive and destructive, but I question whether the liberationists are raising the issue in the most helpful way.[7]

Perhaps more consensus emerges among child advocates when discussion centers around the general, basic rights included in the United Nations Declaration of the Rights of Children or the Rights of Children proposed by the Joint Commission on Mental Health of Children. Particularly in their general form, most would agree with the United Nations that children deserve the right to be "born healthy" or the right to "adequate nutrition, housing, recreation, and medical services." Yet making these rights a reality would require massive social legislation. How many children suffer from malnutrition in the United States, much less worldwide? Thousands of American children suffer from malnutrition even though legislation and money already exist in the form of the Child Nutrition Act.

The 1960 Joint Commission on the Mental Health of Children exposed the sharp discrepancy between children's rights in their general form and the harsh realities of life in America for many children. The commission noted that children should have:

The right to be born healthy, yet approximately 1,000,000 children will be born this year to women who get no medical aid during their pregnancy or no adequate obstetrical care for delivery; thus many will be born with brain damage from disorders of pregnancy. For some, protein and vitamin supplements might have prevented such tragedy.

The right to live in a healthy environment, yet thousands of children and youth become physically handicapped or acquire chronic damage to their health from preventable accidents and diseases, largely because of impoverished environments. Even greater numbers living in poverty will become psychologically handicapped and damaged, unable to compete in school or on a job or to fulfill their inherent capabilities—they will become dependents of, rather than contributors to, our society.

The right to satisfaction of basic needs, yet approximately one-fourth of our children face the probability of malnutrition, inadequate housing, untreated physical and mental disorders, educational handicaps, and indoctrination into a life of marginal work and opportunity.

The right to continuous loving care, yet millions of our young never acquire the necessary motivation or intellectual and emotional skills required to cope effectively in our society because they do not receive consistent, emotionally satisfying care. Society does little to help parents. There are few programs which provide good day care, which aid in developing more adequate child-rearing techniques, or which assist in times of temporary family crisis or where children are neglected or abused.[8]

This bold statement of the rights children should have was made in 1960. Many child advocates could agree with statements written on paper, but making these basic rights a reality in children's lives is the advocates' agenda for the next decades.

What Rights Should Children Not Have?

We have already touched on the question of what rights children should not have. Those who assume that adult rights should not automatically be extended to children would usually oppose giving children the right to vote, the right to earn money and live independently, and the right to sexual freedom. Some would be willing to extend those rights to fifteen-year-olds but not to eight- or ten-year-olds. Age is thus a critical variable in this debate.

Extension of adult rights like legal counsel and full due process procedures to children in divorce, adoption, and foster care decisions is also debated. Opponents claim that those rights for children impinge upon parental rights and allow the state to interfere in basic parent-child relationships. Proponents argue that the risk is worth it in order to safeguard the interests of the child.[9]

'No you may not disobey the law . . . until you grow up.'

There are others who would argue that children should not be given special treatment or special protection under the law, but rather just equal protection under the law. For example, the separate juvenile court system was initially set up to protect children from publicity and possible victimization by juries. Thus, the child's destiny was placed in the hands of the benevolent judge who would presumably act in "the best interests" of the child. Critics of the abuses that prevail in the juvenile court system call for its abolition and for the extension of adult legal rights—namely equal protection and full due process safeguards for the child in the adult court system.[10]

Conflict Among Rights of Children, Parents and the State

The potential for conflict of rights—between the rights of the child and the rights of the parent and between the child's rights and the state's rights is another complex issue.

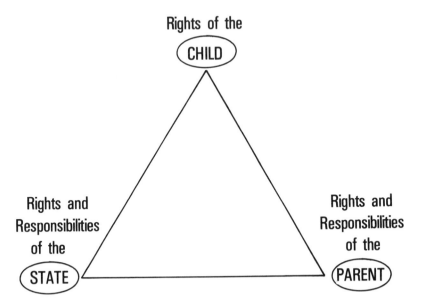

These issues were dramatically raised in the case of four children who had been given up for foster care by their natural mother because of her ill health and emotional difficulties. These four children lived with foster parents for nearly six years and were very happy. However, the natural mother requested that her natural children be returned and the case was taken to court. The foster parents wanted to keep the children, the children wanted to stay with the foster parents, but the natural mother wanted her natural children back. How should the court (representing the interest of the state or society) rule in such a case? What are the best interests of the children? Should the children have their own lawyer? Should their feelings and opinions be admitted as testimony? In this specific case, the judge did not initially consult the children nor did they have a lawyer. The judge ruled that the children must immediately be returned to their natural mother.[11]

John Holt exposes the knotty questions involved with the potential conflict between rights of the state and the child and the parent.

The state cannot guarantee every child a good home and a good family. It does not have these things to give and cannot make or get them. What are its options if it tries to order everyone to make a good home for his child? In the first place, who decides, and on what grounds, whether the home is good? In one case reported in *Life* magazine, the state took children away from their parents, whom they loved and wanted to stay with, because some psychologist had decreed the parents did not have a high enough I.Q. to raise a family—though they had been raising it. In other cases the state has taken unwilling children away from their parents because the neighbors and the community did not approve of the parents' lifestyle or politics. The state can decide things for very peculiar reasons. And if it has been decided, somehow, that the home is not good what does the state do next? Take the child away? Has it other good homes to offer in place of this one? Suppose the child does not want to leave the home, bad as the state thinks it may be? Suppose he likes the old home better than the one the state has provided for him? Suppose he refuses to stay in the "good" home and keeps going back to the old home the state decided wasn't good enough? What happens now is that the state sends the police after him, to take him by force to the home of its choice. Or, if the state does not want to, or cannot, take the child away from a home that it considers bad, does it say to the parents, "This home is bad, make it good"? And if they do not or cannot, what does the state do? Punish them? Will this make the home better?

What we can and should do is leave to the child the right to decide how good his home seems to be and give him the right if he does not like it to choose something else. The state may decide to provide or help provide some of these other choices. But it should not make these choices compulsory. It should allow the child to make choices other than the ones it has provided. It should give the child the right to say no to *it* as well as to his parents.[12]

The Child Versus the Child Advocate

One other critical issue needing thorough examination is, What happens when children exercise their right to question the authority and action of adults who want to be child advocates? How far does the child's right to question and refuse to accept the advice or assistance of the adult advocate go? Are the adults who choose to be child advocates prepared for the possible alienation, criticism, and rejection if "children power" blossoms? Other liberation movements—of blacks, women, and colonized peoples—have had to confront that issue.

Children's rights form a strong basis for action by the child advocate, changing the role of advocate from begging to asserting that the child's needs must be served. Children's rights are gaining the attention of professionals in the fields of education, justice, mental health and retardation, child abuse, health, television and many others. Children's rights to quality services and to due process procedures are the central issues in the debate over the kind of special protection that children need from parents, professionals, and other children. Engaging in that debate is a first step toward changing attitudes and actions affecting America's children.

Notes

1. Lisa Richette, *Throwaway Children*, p. 304.

2. Richette, p. 305.

3. The Honorable Justice Wise Polier, "Myths and Realities in the Search for Juvenile Justice," *The Rights of Children*, Harvard Educational Review, Reprint Series #9, p. 112.

4. All cases referred to were U.S. Supreme Court decisions unless otherwise indicated.

5. I have selected only the most important cases and legislation of that ten-year period. See reference section for books that discuss children's rights in greater detail. Also new cases are constantly going before the Supreme Court. Current periodicals are one way to keep up with recent decisions.

6. Holt, *Escape from Childhood*, p. 110.

7. *Psychology Today*, June 1975, pp. 62-63.

8. Report of the Joint Commission on Mental Health of Children, *Crisis in Child Mental Health: Challenge for the 1970's.*

9. See Joseph Goldstein, Anna Freud and Albert Solnit *Beyond the*

Best Interests of a Child Free Press paperback, 1973, and *Children's Rights Report,* vol. I, no. 4, Dec. 1976-Jan. 1977 and vol. I, no. 6, March 1977.

10.　Martin Guggenheim, *Children's Rights Report,* "A Call to Abolish the Juvenile Justice System," Oct. 1978.

11.　*New York-ex. rel. Wallace* v. *Lhotan.*

12.　Holt, pp. 110-111.

CHAPTER THREE

CHARACTERISTICS OF THE CHILD ADVOCATE

The child advocate is a caring person, a knowledgeable person and an active person. Caring, knowing, and acting are characteristics of the advocate. For discussion and analysis we will separate the three parts of the whole, but caring, knowing, and acting are intertwined and mutually reinforcing.

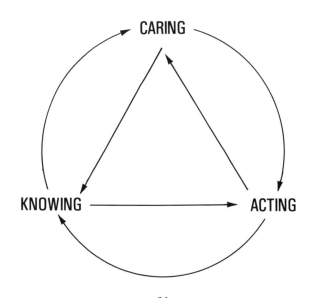

A Child Advocate Cares

While rights can be cited on a time line or in court cases, caring as an essential quality of the advocate is more difficult to delineate. Assessing and being aware of one's own value system is a beginning point.

Reflecting upon one's past actions and decisions is one way to dig into questions like, What do I care about? What do I value? Why? I have found it helpful to reflect upon and even to write out what life experiences and choices have shaped my development as a person. How do I spend my time, energy, and money as a reflection of what I value?

Another dimension of caring is the issue of commitment. In my experience, there are no quick, final solutions to most of the problems dealt with by child advocates. Nor is there any perfect human social system. Rather, child advocacy is a continuing process needing commitment to long-term as well as to short-term change.

Finding and accepting support and inspiration from others is an essential resource. Many times I have felt discouraged or directionless and have found renewed focus and energy from coworkers, from a powerful speech, or from an article about the efforts of an advocacy group.

What keeps caring from edging over to paternalism or "child saving"? Since the child advocate is acting on behalf of a powerless group—children—the danger of the adult's own needs being confused with the best interests of children is always present. "We must imprison the child for his own good." "I hit my child to teach him what's right." "We must drug the hyperactive child before we can teach him." These kinds of statements are heard all too often in America today.

The child advocate must wrestle with questions like, What are my interests and motivations? When are my concerns, interests, and perceptions the same as the best interests of the children I am helping and at what times are they divergent? Am I enabling and empowering children to be their own advocates?

Caring can be soured easily in American society by powerful

voices offering individualistic solutions and urging us to "blame the victim." William Ryan has incisively exposed and analyzed the ways that an ideology of blaming the victim pervades American social service systems.[1] It is easy to blame children themselves for being poor, illiterate or ungovernable rather than looking at the systems and institutions that are failing to help children develop. It is easy for staff people in agencies to blame parents and say, "I can't do anything with that child if his own parents don't even care." It is easy for parents to scapegoat a single teacher or caseworker rather than look at the multiple causes of institutional failure.

Advocates are aware of the potential power in their own roles and their own complicity in maintaining the status quo. The advocate wrestles with questions such as:

1. What power do I have in my roles as parent, staff person, neighbor or citizen?
2. How far does my responsibility extend?
3. What forces go beyond my role and control, and how can I enlist the support and action of those persons and groups who do have the power to make those changes?

A Child Advocate Knows

A child advocate must know enough to make his/her caring effective. An advocate must know the facts of a specific case and must know what results are wanted in a particular agency or on a particular project. Child advocates must know how the system or systems that they work with function and how to impact upon them. They must know how to document facts and evidence.[2] They must understand the rights of children.[3] They must be aware of resources and what other child advocates and organizations are doing.[4]

The *Oakes Newsletter* illustrates how one person has used her skills and caring to enable others to know more about the Philadelphia School System so that they can act more effectively. Helen Oakes, the author and publisher, had been active as a parent of four children in the turbulent 1960s and 1970s. She was a member and leader of several community organizations like the West Philadelphia Schools Committee and the Citizens' Committee for Public Education. In the late 1960s, she assessed her skills and commitment and the needs of the advocacy groups working in public education. She decided that a well-researched monthly newsletter, which would be read by a wide cross section of the community, would be a lever for change. The first issue was published in April 1970. The newsletter is financed by subscriptions and a few foundation grants. It is mailed to 2,100 people, including all school principals, members of the school board, presidents of parents' associations, building representatives of the Teachers' Union, and education editors of newspapers and radio and television. It has an impact upon the Philadelphia School System because it provides well-researched information for parents and citizen advocacy organizations and because critical issues are identified for concerned policymakers and school personnel.

One *Oakes Newsletter* told the story of Floyd Logan, who persisted over a forty-year period working for changes in the public school system. Helen Oakes thinks he "merits our deep respect for his integrity, singleness of purpose, refusal to be turned from his course and sacrifices for a cause." Note that Floyd Logan used a variety of methods in addition to litigation to change the system. He used his individual strengths and skills through an organization that he had founded. He focused on specific issues in one system and persisted until he saw significant changes in the system.

The Oakes Newsletter

An Independent Monthly Dedicated
To Improving Public Education.
Helen Oakes—Author and Publisher

Floyd Logan—a Lifetime Devoted to a Cause[5]

Many people have heard of Floyd Logan and the Educational Equality League, but there are probably very

few who know, understand and appreciate the tremendously significant contribution that he has made to public
education in Philadelphia and other parts of Pennsylvania. For forty-three years, Floyd Logan has fought
tenaciously and effectively against discrimination prac-
ticed against students and School District employees, for
the promotion of democratic representation on the
School Board and for the desegregation of schools in and
out of Philadelphia. Though he is now in his 70's, he
continues his untiring efforts.

I write this Newsletter for paradoxical reasons. On the
one hand, more people should know that, because of the
ceaseless efforts of the Educational Equality League,
Philadelphia is far ahead of most northern big city school
systems in the percentage of black women and men in
positions of decision making, leadership and major
responsibility at the school, administrative and school
board levels. Without the League's early and continuing
pressure, this would not have come about.

Who is this man that has been President and an
effective leader of the Educational Equality League for
forty-three years? Floyd Logan grew up in Asheville,
North Carolina and came to Philadelphia in 1921. He
worked for the U.S. Customs Service and then for the
Internal Revenue Service until medical reasons forced
him to take advantage of an optional retirement program
in 1955.

Down through the years, the League has utilized many
avenues in the pursuit of its goals. It has gone to the
courts many times. Floyd Logan has written thousands of
carefully thought out, expressive letters to presidents,
governors, mayors, boards of education and school
superintendents. He has pointed out injustices, asked for
corrective measures and always been factual, firm, polite
and restrained. He has shunned histrionics and used
statistics, logic, documented facts, analyses of School
District reports and a methodical approach to achieve
breakthroughs and improvements. He has developed

good working relationships with board members, superintendents and top administrators and has proceeded to right all kinds of wrong through the practice of quiet, dogged, personal diplomacy.

Floyd Logan and his wife have lived first on his modest income and then on his pension—circumstances which might have caused a lesser man to have allowed himself to be bought off long ago. He has had no connection with the school system, so he has never had anything personal to gain from his efforts and he has always kept his independence.

Mr. Logan began his crusade in 1932 with a successful effort to remove an objectionable social studies textbook from the schools. According to the newspaper accounts written at the time, he led a committee of sixteen "colored organizations" representing 110,000 citizens who wrote to the President of the Board of Education objecting to the use of this book which they said disseminated propaganda against Negroes. The textbook was removed from the approved list.

Not long after that incident he formally organized the Educational Equality League and it began its struggle against the flagrant discrimination and segregation that existed in the Philadelphia school system. There were twelve elementary schools in the city at that time in which all of the pupils, teachers and principals were black. All of the black teachers in the system taught in these schools. No black teachers taught in secondary schools. No black teachers taught white children in any school. The school board had no blacks on it. Other than teachers, the School District employed very few black men and women and only in the lowest paying jobs. There were no black professionals in secondary schools or central administrations.

It was Mr. Logan and the Educational Equality League that undertook the early, difficult and highly significant battles for representation on the school board, the break-down on the color line at all levels in employment and the integration of the students in the schools. It is a credit to his faith and perseverance that he has kept at it all these years and a tragedy that the history of the struggle is full of delays, postponements and foot dragging.

Steps Forward

One of the first efforts of the Educational Equality League was a campaign to get a black member appointed to the Board of Education. It resulted in the appointment of Dr. John P. Turner, a police surgeon, to the Board in 1935. He served as the sole black representative on the fifteen member Board for twenty-three years, until his death in 1958. His seat was then filled by the now deceased E. Washington Rhodes, a lawyer and the publisher of the Philadelphia *Tribune*. It wasn't until 1962, when Robert W. Williams Jr. was appointed, that the Board had two black members. Black representation increased to three for the first time in 1971.

In the mid-30's, the Educational Equality League began the struggle to have black teachers appointed to the secondary schools and to abolish the racially separate lists of eligible teachers which had resulted in black teachers being assigned to teach only black children. The League proposed a program of "experimental appointments" to secondary schools and achieved the first one in 1935 when a black art teacher was appointed to the previously all white faculty at Sulzberger Junior High School. The lists were merged in 1937. It took extra courage and stamina to work for the merging of the lists, because this was not universally supported by black teachers. Many believed that this would lead to a drop in the number of jobs for blacks. However, in time, the abandonment of the dual lists did lead to desegregation of staffs in all schools and therefore more jobs for blacks. Floyd Logan's stand on the lists was consistent with the way he works. He took a principled position and stayed with it, popular or not.

It was 1946, eleven years after the junior high school appointment, before a black teacher was appointed to a senior high school. (See table below.) Ten years after that, there were less than sixty black teachers in senior high and vocational-technical schools. There were no black department heads and only one black principal. You can see how slowly things have moved in the high schools from 1946 to the present. Although the numbers have improved, they are still well below what they should be, especially for teachers and department heads.

When statistics like these are brought forward, school administrators often reply that not enough black people are qualified for these positions for promotion. It is important to remember that to the extent that this is true, the School District bears responsibility. For many years, very few black people prepared to go into secondary education, because there were *no* employment opportunities in it in Philadelphia. Also, it was not until very recently, as the chart shows, that there have been promotional opportunities for blacks in high schools.

The Educational Equality League has worked consistently for the promotion of blacks to top administrative levels of the school district. On two occasions in the early and mid-60s, there were a number of important positions to be filled. The School District tried to ignore the demands of the Educational Equality League and others to give equal consideration to the advancement of blacks, but they were finally forced to promote blacks to some of the top level openings. If the Educational Equality League had not been at work many years earlier there would not have been people in significant administrative positions to move into these top level openings.

The Educational Equality League has worked steadily for student integration inside and outside the city. Back in 1934, Floyd Logan was involved with securing admission of black pupils into a new school in Berwyn from which they had been excluded. The League worked to desegregate Chester schools, Girard College, and the

Milton Hershey School in Hershey, Pa. and intensified its efforts to integrate the state's public school systems after the 1954 Supreme Court decision. Floyd Logan's efforts made him a target of hate mail and phone calls. He also received threats on his life which were taken so seriously by the authorities that on more than one occasion he was assigned police protection.

Space does not permit describing many of the diverse problems and policies that the League has grappled with over the years. They have varied from the ending of segregated classes in hair dressing in the vocational-technical schools to working for increased employment of black non-instructional personnel. While the League's major emphasis has been on the problems of blacks in the system, it has also served as advocate for members of other minority groups when they were subject to discrimination. . . .

Floyd Logan merits our deep respect for his integrity, singleness of purpose, refusal to be turned from his course and sacrifice for a cause.

Sr. High & Voc-Tech. Schools	1946	1956	1966	Dec. 1974
Black Teachers	1	58	333 (14%)	21%
Black Department Heads	0	0	1	16%
Black Principals	0	1	1	28%

In addition to the Newsletter, Helen Oakes has published *A Statistical Analysis: A School by School Survey,* which gives information on racial distribution of students, absentee rates of students and staff, reading scores of each school, and numbers of experienced teachers in each school. Having this kind of information about all 280 schools in one easy-to-read booklet, the advocate has access to facts that can be the basis for asking questions. If, for example, an advocate asks a school principal, "How well are the children at this school reading?" a vague, meaningless answer is, "Oh, the children are achieving well." If the advocate knows the exact reading scores, a more precise follow-up question could refer to those facts—"What are you doing to help the thirty percent of the children who are reading below the sixteenth percentile?" That kind of question will usually produce a more specific and substantive answer from the school official.

Knowing facts and doing solid homework are a must for the advocate.

A Child Advocate Acts

Knowing is closely bound up with acting and reflecting on previous work and experience. The intertwining of caring, knowing, and acting is reflected in the advocate's approach of acting out of a commitment to the children he/she is connected to, of using facts as the basis for action, and using action to uncover more facts.

It is essential to begin with the roles and situations where we find ourselves rather than waiting for the perfect moment, the foolproof strategy or the charismatic leader. Ways to plan effective action are discussed in the next chapter, as well as a variety of action strategies useful to advocates.

Gerri Chester: An Effective Child Advocate

The characteristics of caring, knowing and acting are illustrated by Gerri Chester, who says she felt like a "nobody from nowhere" when she first became involved to help her handicapped child. Now she is known throughout the state of Colorado as a child advocate and the founder of the Colorado Society for Autistic Children and the Colorado Council of Organizations for the Handicapped. Her case advocacy on behalf of her own son led her to class advocacy and changing systems.

She shared her story with other parents at the Second National Conference on Parental Involvement in 1977.[6]

I was up against what seemed to be an impossible task. In fact, if I had known what obstacles I would have to overcome, I probably wouldn't have had the courage to start in the first place, BUT . . .

My son needed help! After four-and-a-half traumatic years of evaluation, he was finally diagnosed as autistic. I was told I had two choices: put him in an institution or find a special school program for him. I decided on the school program—no one bothered to tell me there was none. This I discovered by talking to every special education director of every school district and the head of every agency in the state. They all gave me the same story: no program, no money to start one, don't know what to do about autism, anyway.

Just when I began to feel like I had the only autistic child in the world, I found out about the National Society for Autistic Children. They advised me not to move but to fight it out in Colorado. Articles about my situation in the Sunday magazine sections of both local newspapers put me in touch with hundreds of helpful people as well as parents of other autistic children.

We formed the Colorado Chapter of NSAC and launched a major assault on the system. I took my son to the neighborhood school and left him with the first grade teacher. I assured her that even though he didn't talk much and acted a little bizarre, he would be all right if she locked the door so he couldn't escape. The social worker called me and gently broke the news that the school had a problem with my son. I laughed all the way back to school because I knew it must be crumbling around their ears.

I insisted that if they have had programs for retarded children in the schools, they must have some place for my son. Again, they told me there was nothing available.

I found out the schools were supported by property taxes and refused to pay mine. I returned a letter with my tax bill advising that I did not intend to pay my taxes until my son was served by a school program. I sent copies to the Governor, the Joint Budget Committee and the Commissioner of Education. I also told them I was ready to go to court anytime they were. I didn't pay taxes for four years, and state officials never challenged me. I was rather hoping they would.

The social worker from the local school asked me to sign a form relieving the Denver Public Schools of the responsibility for educating my son. When I refused, she assured me that it was a standard, very harmless form and my refusal to sign would accomplish nothing. She chased me around for ten months. I felt it must be important or she wouldn't be so determined to get it signed. Then I advised all other parents not to sign a form either.

I decided to take the matter of the form up with the school board. I told them I would sign *their* form relieving them of the responsibility for my son's education if they would sign *my* form agreeing to pay my son's private school tuition of $800 per month. They refused but I never saw their form again.

The next year I tried again to register my son for school, just to let them know I was still around. When he was refused, I withdrew registration for my two daughters. I was told I was violating a compulsory attendance law by keeping them out of school.

I asked how they could force me to send my daughters to school and deny school to my son under the same law. I told them the law was obviously unconstitutional so I didn't mind violating it.

During the course of my well-publicized battle, the Governor wrote and asked me to visit his office. I gave him my list of all the people and agencies I had contacted trying to get help for my son. He responded by appointing a task force to investigate the problem of autism and make recommendations. After almost a year, the task force recommended the first public school program for autistic children in the state's history. The year was 1970.

Today, because of a handful of parents with nothing going for them but guts and determination, Special Education is serving over 80,000 handicapped children in Colorado and is funded at $33 million—not quite what we requested for full implementation of the law but it is certainly a great improvement over the $3.5 million in 1965.

In addition to caring, knowing and acting, Gerri Chester had a willingness to take some risks, flexibility, an ability to learn from mistakes, and perhaps—most critical of all—*persistence*.

Notes

1. See *Blaming the Victim*, William Ryan, Vintage, 1971.
2. See chapter Four on Fact-finding Skills.
3. See chapter Two.
4. See Resources Section, chapter Nine.
5. *The Oakes Newsletter* (vol. VI, no. 5, Jan 28, 1975), 6400 Drexel Rd., Phila., Pa. 19151. Floyd Logan died in 1979.
6. From her speech "Becoming Involved" reprinted in *Network*, February 1978, published by the National Committee for Citizens in Education.

SKILLS OF THE CHILD ADVOCATE

Child advocates must be able to find the facts, plan strategies, develop effective groups, and negotiate with officials. These four skills are vital.

Finding the Facts

Knowledge is power. Getting and using information is the basis for effective action. Fact-finding is a must.

Asking questions is the first step. Some fundamental questions the advocate will ask of the system he/she is trying to influence include:

Who controls decision making?

What is the formal power structure?

What is the informal power structure?

Who controls the budget or who sets priorities for use of money?

How does the political system impact upon the system or agency?

What rights do children have in this system?

What rights do parents have?

What rights do employees have?

What rights do employers and policymakers have?

What are the channels for complaints or grievances?

74

Who are actual or potential change agents within the system? Outside the system?
What are the sources of resistance to change in the institutions?

Make Maps of the System

The advocate first asks the relevant questions but then must begin to uncover the answers. The first question, "Who controls the decision making?" is a good place to begin. Many systems and agencies have an organizational chart that illustrates the formal decision-making structure. For example, the formal structure of most school systems conforms to this sample organizational chart. The board of education, whether elected or appointed, is the policy-making body that hires the superintendent and other employees to carry out those policies.

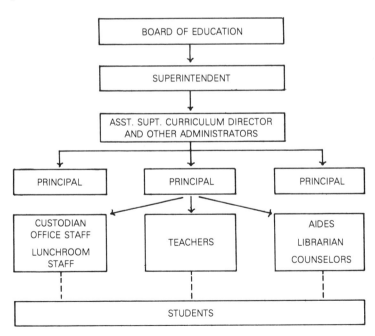

Who's Who in the System

This chart can be used to figure out who wields the power in the system. A group of advocates can pool their knowledge at one of their planning meetings and fill in the blanks with names and titles of key people.

FORMAL DECISION-MAKERS

POLICY BOARD

↓

ADMINISTRATORS

↓

DIRECT SERVICE
PERSONNEL

↓

CHILDREN BEING
SERVED

THE REAL DECISION-MAKERS

THE KEY DECISION-MAKERS

↓

THE IMPLEMENTORS

↓

THE "YES" PEOPLE WHO DO WHAT THEY'RE TOLD

↓

THE EXCLUDED OR IGNORED

Talk to People Who Know

Who can give you information about a system? One source is the system's *officials*. It is wise to make requests for information in writing and to keep carbon copies of the request. Do not be put off by vague answers or professional jargon. If you do not get a clear answer, ask the question again, as specifically and directly as possible. If you are dealing with a public agency, remember that the officials are public servants and have a responsibility to inform you.

Another major source of information about a system is its *consumers*—the children and families that the system was set up to serve. Conversations with children and their parents are invaluable as are more formal surveys of the opinions and feelings of the consumer.

Front line employees also have a wealth of information about how the system actually works. Since the teacher, nurse, child-care worker, and ward attendant are at the point where services are delivered to the children, they all know the system from a special vantage point.

See for Yourself

Fact-finding usually requires first-hand observation, which involves asking questions, but also looking and listening intently. There is no substitute for firsthand observation of the system in action. See for yourself what children are experiencing by visiting the school, courtroom, jail, mental hospital, or clinic.

The following article by Arlene Silberman indicates the importance of observation.

What Should Parents Look for in Their Children's Schools?

by Arlene Silberman

Four years and 50,000 miles ago, I first began to learn what good schools can and should be like. As a mother of four school-age sons, with a master's degree from Teachers College, Columbia University, and years of teaching experience, I thought I already knew. . . . Three continents and countless classrooms later, I can finally answer all the parents who ask, "How can I tell if my child's school is doing a good job? . . . "

There are only three requirements for a good elementary school:

1. A pleasant atmosphere in which every child feels valued and successful.
2. A faculty concerned with developing youngsters who delight in learning.
3. Programs that respond to each child's individual needs.

Let's visit a school teacher so you'll know how to spot the clues that tell you if the combination is working.

We'll start early because you'll get your first inkling in the school yard as the children arrive. Do they enter the building freely, as they do at home, or must they line up like soldiers awaiting orders? Too many schools forget that they are a child's home for most of the day, not a military base. If we see youngsters locked out in the icy wind, we'll know to look for other signs of insensitivity in this school.

You may wonder if the pleasant atmosphere really matters. I am convinced it does, for if a child's early experiences are distasteful, he may decide that learning, like medicine, is only to be taken in a small dose when absolutely necessary. In that case, his school has failed. I can say flatly that I have never seen a good school within a harsh environment.

We'll find our next clue in the hallways. Bare walls suggest a school that is barren in other ways, too. Good schools typically burst with paintings, posters and murals because they know that children are creative creatures whose talents and love of beauty will grow if properly nurtured. They also know that children can express feelings through art that they may not be able to put into words. What's more, even the least able student feels successful when he sees his painting on display. Art, in sum, is essential to a good elementary school.

Our next step is the outer office. While we're there,

notice if the principal keeps his door open (except during private conferences) so that he can hear the pulsebeat of his school. Later we'll see if he remains closeted away or if he visits classes and chats with children in the halls. You'll know he doesn't emerge often if he calls every girl "Sweetheart" and every boy "Son." I always like the principal who asks Ida (by name) about her baby sister and Bill (by name) about his latest Scout badge. . . .

Your principal is the key to your school. If he views himself as an administrator, wrapped up in lunch schedules and absence notes, the school may be efficient, but don't expect much more. But if he views himself as an educator, a teacher of teachers and children, chances are he runs a good school.

The tip-off to whether you're with an administrator or an educator is the question, "What do you see as your goals?" If he replies with the curriculum he wants covered, grade by grade, you're not talking with an educator; if he talks about the attitudes and abilities he tries to foster in his children, you probably are, for educators know that *how* a child feels about learning is as important as *what* he learns. Repeating what the teachers and textbooks say is one thing; having the initiative to raise questions and the know-how to explore new areas independently is quite another. The first is memorizing; the second, learning it's important not to confuse the two. . . .

Don't make the mistake of thinking that reading scores tell the whole story, however. I did, until a London headmistress set me straight. "I'll gladly show you our reading scores," she replied to my question, "but first I must point out that *what* my children read concerns me as much as how well they read. Too many competent readers develop into adults who read trash. I want my youngsters to enjoy poetry and drama, fiction and biography—and you won't discover that from test scores." How right she was!

Since we'll make most of our discoveries in the

classroom, let's visit as many as we can. We may be given a list of rooms that are open to us. Does the teacher greet us at the door as we enter, or does she pretend that we are phantoms, silent and invisible? Do the children glance at us furtively, not daring to let their eyes meet ours, much less risking to say "hello" or to have us greet them? Those are all signs of a tense, unnatural environment where normal sociability is forbidden. A similar sign is the requirement that children ask permission to sharpen a pencil or throw a piece of paper away.

Keep listening to the sounds of the room. In a good classroom you may hear laughing and squeals of delight as children suddenly grasp a new idea or make an unexpected discovery; you may hear groans of disappointment if an experiment doesn't work out. And you may hear conversation as children help one another. But you won't encounter long periods of silence, except during a test. Nor will you hear the teacher doing 70 to 80 percent of the talking (which is about average, according to research studies), because the children will be participating more.

As you listen, count the number of times the teacher says "no" or an equivalent put-down. Teachers who hear tape recordings of themselves are often shocked to learn how negative they sound. "No wonder half my class never volunteers," a young teacher confessed after listening to herself. "I've crushed them! . . ."

Be alert to what happens if a child gives a correct answer that doesn't happen to be the one the teacher wanted. Does the teacher brush it aside because she is determined to follow her lesson plan? Or does she accept the unexpected learning opportunity? . . .

A good school finds ways of individualizing the program. At least a thousand classrooms have completely abandoned the usual approach of having a teacher instruct the entire class as a unit. Instead, students work individually or in small groups, according to their interests and skills, while the teacher circulates about the room, helping a few children at a time, knowing that the others are proceeding independently or helping each other. In the same class, Sally may still be learning to write simple sentences, while Jill is already composing intricate stories. Neither has to be skipped or left back. And any child who has been absent simply picks up where he left off. . . .

Many rooms have a gold star chart. Too many, for the stars are not merely a way of rewarding the successful, but also a way of labeling the failures. "I don't have a lot of stars because I'm dumb in arithmetic" (or spelling, or reading—I heard them all). And the tearful child who whispers this confession uses a very different tone of voice from the youngster who is eager for me to see his impressive collection of gold stars. Since we know that a child who senses he has been labeled a failure often lives up to that expectation, it's essential to build his self-esteem, not chip away at it.

There is something worthwhile in every school, and you would do well to compliment people on the things that please you. They will appreciate the fact that you have not come to debunk all of their efforts. Then single out two or three things that trouble you most.

No school can measure up in every way, of course, but every school can be helped to do a better job. You can begin to help your child's school by getting to know it well. Don't limit your visits to one or two classrooms during Open School Week. And go with an open mind—and with open eyes and ears. . . . [1]

Research Varied Sources

Fact-finding skills also include searching for background information on the system the child advocate is working within or attempting to influence. Some of that information may be gotten from informal conversations or formal interviews with people working within the community. Newspapers and magazine articles are also good sources. Many advocate groups have newsletters to provide vital data.

The system that a child advocate is focusing on may also publish important information including surveys, studies, and evaluations. The federal Freedom of Information law and "sunshine laws" in many states guarantee citizens the right to examine and make copies of public records of public agencies. If needed information is not already published by the institution or system, the child advocate can make a formal request for the information. The request should be in writing.

Sunshine laws in most states require that decisions made by public agencies be made in meetings open to the public. Thus policy and budgets are a part of the public record. School boards, boards of public agencies, state and local elected bodies hold public meetings, and records of meetings may even be on tape or transcribed.

Research can be valuable but it is usually a time-consuming, long-range project. Child advocates in local communities frequently can turn to state or national organizations for research information or assistance with research.[2] The Children's Defense Fund researches specific issues that affect children in local communities throughout the country. C.D.F. then publishes the findings, develops specific policy recommendations, and offers the data and support to local advocacy groups.[3]

Keep Written Records

In addition to collecting new facts from all available sources, advocates should also keep carefully written records of their actions because they become part of the facts of the case. Keep a log of all telephone calls and letters to officials, and be sure to record date and time. After a meeting with an official, the advocate should write a *letter of understanding* of what occurred at the meeting. It can be as simple as this: "My understanding of the issues discussed and agreements reached at the meeting on (date and time) were _____ and _____. Present at the meeting were (list names of advocates and officials).

Wherever they are, find the facts. Knowledge is power and the key to effective advocacy is using power to act on behalf of children.

Basic Guidelines for Case Advocacy

1. *Know your facts.* Be sure they are correct. Find out: Who? What? Where? When? and Why?
2. *Know the rights* of the child, the parent, or other parties in the case. Contact an advocacy organization or lawyer if you have any questions.
3. *Know the policy* and/or procedures that relate to the problem. Get it in writing, don't just accept a verbal version.
4. *Keep accurate notes.* Document as much evidence as possible. Date everything.
5. *Discuss various options* with the child or parents you are assisting. Do not tell the young person or parent what to do. Rather let the person (child or parent) *choose* the option and course of action that is wisest and that he/she is willing to live with.
6. *Never go alone* (except in unusual circumstances) to a meeting with officials. Take the young person, the parent, or other concerned person with you.
7. In meeting with officials, *keep to the point,* be firm but not antagonistic, keep focused on the problem and the need for a resolution of the problem. Try to steer clear of personalities.
8. *Follow channels.* Don't go over a person's head until you have seen him/her about the problem. It is wise to let that person know you are dissatisfied with the result of your meeting and that you intend to go to the next person in authority.
9. If appropriate, send a letter to indicate your understanding of what took place at a meeting with officials or administrators.

Planning Action

Child advocates need skills in planning action, as well as fact-finding skills. Some of the steps in planning that a group of child advocates can follow are these:

1. Identify the problems.
2. Select one problem to work on.
3. Set an action goal.
4. Identify and choose strategies or types of action to achieve that goal.
5. Evaluate the effectiveness of the strategy for achieving the action goal.

I will focus this discussion on a *group* planning process because a group can often be more effective than a single advocate, especially for systems change. Also many advocates have had less experience in group advocacy, perhaps due to the strong tradition of individualism and casework in the United States. The steps outlined are nonetheless applicable for case advocacy, too.

Since planning action is such an essential skill for the child advocate, let's go back and look at some specific suggestions under each of these steps that a group of child advocates could follow.[4]

1. List the most pressing problem(s). Find out what your concerns are, where the problem(s) lies. Listen to each other.

   Ask each member of the group to help brainstorm to discover problems. Do not stop to discuss each problem—just briefly state it and write it out on a blackboard or on a sheet of paper large enough so that everyone can see it. (This helps focus the group discussion so that it does not turn into a "gripe" session.)

2. Select one problem to zero in on and agree to work as a group to solve one problem at a time.

   Since a group cannot solve every problem immediately,

make an agreement to work together to set priorities and concentrate efforts.

On a separate sheet of paper or on the blackboard, list the following:
Criteria that the group can use for selecting the main issue.

a. Is it a problem that is urgent?

   It is easier to generate feeling and action around an urgent, highly visible problem. It's a good beginning spot.

b. Is it a problem that unites the members in the group?

   Avoid divisive issues, especially when the group is new. Instead, select issues on which there is basic agreement.

c. Is it a problem that this group of advocates can do something about?

d. Is it a problem that interests me (each one in the group)?

   Solving the problem should give every member of the group some "payoff," in the sense that everyone feels gratification or sees some evidence of an improved situation for children. Those group members who don't get some satisfaction out of working on the problem will drop out sooner or later.

e. Is it a problem that is OK for me and for this group to work on?

   If working on the problem raises conflict of interest questions for too many members, they may quietly back off. If conflicts exist, they would have to be very honestly and directly discussed before selecting it as the first problem.

f. Is it a problem that is winnable? Can we succeed in a reasonably short period of time?

   Win some small, specific changes—then tackle some of the harder ones. Solving a problem builds group solidarity and provides the momentum to attack tough problems.

g. Is the problem a symptom or a root cause of low quality services for children?

Sometimes a new group deliberately will decide to work on a problem that is a symptom rather than a root cause because it is usually easier to cure a symptom. However, the group should be aware of this, and should not be under the illusion that curing the symptom will solve the fundamental problems.

3. Set the action goal. It is vital for the group to state and agree on two major points:

What you want changed.

When you want it changed.

After you have selected the main problem to be worked on you may need to *assign people to get additional facts* before setting the *action goal* and *plan of* action.

The same criteria for selecting the problem listed above should be used to define and zero in on the action goal.

An example of an action goal is: "By June 10, this advocate group will secure emergency clothing allowances for the 95 children displaced by the Stoney Creek flood."

Defining an action goal is no easy task, and as the group begins to get more specific and move toward a plan of action, disagreement may surface. The group may need to pause and reassess:

Is everyone clear why *this* action goal should be pursued? Can everyone still "buy into" trying to solve it? Is the action goal specific enough to produce some results fairly soon?

4. Plan strategies and types of action to achieve the goal. Develop a short-range set of action plans—concrete first steps and more generalized next steps.

Fact-finding is usually the first step in a plan of action. It serves to acquaint members of the group to plan the best strategy. Do not get locked into a plan of action that does not consider new information.

Discuss alternative ways to resolve the problems and brainstorm a list of strategies that could be used.

Then *choose an action* plan that will secure the most immediate results. How many times have you been in groups where the first and only suggestion for action is to write a letter? Advocates need to have readily available a variety of types of action: writing, calling, or visiting policy-makers; holding public hearings and community meetings; monitoring programs and meetings, resorting to sit-ins, phone-ins, and talk-ins or even boycotts, strikes, or court injunctions.

The *plan of action* should be very specific, with people assigned to specific tasks, with dates and times clearly agreed upon, with flexibility and a chance to report back and agree upon next steps.

Each time the group meets, the following should be discussed:
   What *new information* do we have that affects our plan of action?
   What do we need to *know* or *do* next?
   Who will take responsibility for each task?
   When do we want these tasks accomplished?
If these questions are asked, no one will leave a meeting that has been "just talk," and no action.
5. Evaluate your effectiveness.
   Evaluating is simply finding out what has happened. What have we accomplished? What do we need to do next?
   Get regular *feedback* from the group by asking:
        How are we doing as a group?
        Is everyone in agreement with what we're doing?
        What did we do that was effective?
        What mistakes did we make?

Self-evaluation is important for building a strong group. As much as 20 percent of the group's time should be allowed for this kind of feedback. It helps the group see where it is. It gives members a chance to air feelings (positive and negative) directly in the group instead of "back-biting" over the telephone or after the meeting.

This may seem risky and scary at first; you may be afraid that conflict and disagreement will split the group. But in fact, groups are more likely to dissolve if hurt feelings or differences of opinion are ignored or allowed to fester under the surface—with some people dropping out or others hanging on until there's a "blow-out."

A number of negative feelings may surface. But don't be surprised at the positive ones. You're also likely to hear:

I see now that I need a group if I'm to be effective;

I've learned how to ask the right questions;

I used to think no one else cared. I see now that's not true. Feedback is a necessity, not a frill.

The variety of actions identified and briefly discussed below give the advocate a rich "grab bag" of ideas. Find the type of action that will most effectively solve the problem.

These are excerpts from *Let Our Children Go* by Douglas Biklen of the Syracuse Center on Human Policy. See his book for a detailed and useful "how to do it" section with examples along with each type of action.

Public Hearings & Fact Finding Forums

Fact finding forums include: citizen investigation panels; town meetings; community polls; seminars by expert panels; and TV question and answer programs.

Purpose

Fact finding panels and meetings can help to identify community needs, but they can also serve as an action. Any citizen can give testimony (usually five or ten minutes worth) before legislative panels, town councils, and county legislatures. These formats may not adequately meet your objectives, however, in which case you could set up your own public hearings.

The self initiated town meeting or citizen investigation focuses attention on your issues . . . and, more often than not, the town meeting is the first of a series of actions for social change.

Public hearings help you go on record. They can also be used to force a confrontation.

Letter Writing

When people think of letter writing they think of the "letter to your Congressman." Actually, letter writing can include other effective forms: carbon copies to attorneys; public letters; leaflets; letters to editors; skywriting; newsletters; letter-bulletins; letters of support to groups that share your interests; letters of complaint; letters to create a record.

Purpose

Advocates often send letters to administrators, with carbon copies of these letters to a sympathetic lawyer. This pressures the bureaucrats.

Letters serve as a formal record. When you have achieved a victory or precedent in agency policy, you can document this by sending the administrator a letter that says, "It is my understanding that you have agreed to do the following. . . ."

Following a conversation with your opposition, you may want to record your view of the conversation in a letter to them. This way, you force them to respond in writing: either they agree with your interpretation of the conversation or they must deny it.

If you receive letters from your opposition, these may help your cause; you may want to publish them in your newsletter or offer them to the local press.

Letters can serve as a format for organizing groups to mobilize pressure against a particular service agency.

Community Education

Workshops; teach-ins; consciousness-raising groups; consumer meetings; speakers bureaus; speeches; posters and newspapers.

Purpose

Every action that you undertake will have an educational value. Hence, you should try to get the most out of your actions by preparing educational materials, newsletters, press releases, workshops and manuals.

Workshops or teach-ins help build skills among consumer groups. Workshops help to educate the constituency and they also create a sense of group spirit among consumers. A workshop or teach-in is a good way to bring together different groups; workshops also highlight community needs. When hundreds of parents attend a workshop on legal rights, for example, the community at large will realize that legal rights are an "issue" to be reckoned with.

Model Programs

Group homes; integrated day care; vocational training; information and referral; special education.

Purpose

If you can demonstrate alternatives to current service systems, people will begin to think of change as practical and possible. The creation of alternative social institutions often forces existing institutions to change.

The great danger of model programs is that the social change organization will turn into a service provider and lose its status as organizer and advocate. If your group becomes a service provider, you will probably not help to promote change. Rather, you take pressure off of the other service agencies because you are providing the services that they should provide.

If there is a need for new service agencies in the community, you should organize these separately from your advocacy program so as not to confuse advocating with providing direct services. *The advocate monitors human services but does not provide them.*

Symbolic Acts

Perhaps the most fun of all the organizing tactics is the symbolic act. Mock awards; mock elections; mock public hearings; street theatre; mock events.

Purpose

The symbolic act calls attention, often sarcastically, to a policy or practice or need that deserves exposure. The refusal of an award, for example, can focus attention on the event and an issue. Because it appears shocking or unusual, the symbolic act is talked about long after the action has occurred.

Demonstrations

Demonstrations are a form of public communication that has been used by the women's suffrage movement, the civil rights movement, and other human rights struggles. Types of demonstrations include: marches; vigils; sit-ins; phone-ins; jam-ins; sing-ins; leafleting; and picketing.

Purpose

Demonstrations publicize your issue. They are an easy, successful, short-term type of action that have the added effect of creating a sense of group purpose and accomplishment. Demonstrations are a tactic for monitoring institutions, social service agencies, schools, and courts. Demonstrations are a "community presence."

Communication

In addition to newsletters and town meetings, advocates must utilize a variety of communication networks and media: booklets; pamphlets; seminars; workshops; slide shows; movies; resource guides; press conferences; TV debates; radio shows; exposés; phoning campaigns; advertisements; public service announcements; press releases.

Purpose

Communications are the heart of any organizing effort. In order to change policies and practices, we must change attitudes.

We need to develop a variety of materials for communication, including slide presentations, resource booklets on the needs and rights of children, educational materials, newsletters, and action bulletins.

Communications help to educate your supporters and the broader community. Newsletters keep people informed about recent events, successes, and meetings.

Communications serve as the ongoing symbol that the group exists and will act again in the future.

The news release and press conference are two essential communication formats. Whenever your group achieves a victory, launches a campaign, reacts to a policy or practice, makes an announcement, or plans an action, the press should be notified. If you have a guest speaker from out of town, always arrange a press conference with newspapers and TV cameras present.

Lobbying

Lobbying may mean pushing for legislative change or administrative policy change. You can use several tactics, including: phone calls; petitions; alternative budgets and alternative plans; telegram campaigns; and public statements.

Purpose

Lobbying helps change the laws and policies so that they better meet your needs.

Lobbying can educate legislators and the public about your issues.

Lobbying involves masses of people in large campaigns. This helps to solidify your movement and to create a feeling of strength.

Lobbying always makes the lobbyists more informed about current laws and policies and about how political leaders vote on key issues. This information can be shared with the organizing group and with the community at large.

Boycotts

Boycott; strike; non-cooperation; slow compliance; stalling; refusal to pay for services; and work-ins.

Purpose

The boycott is a familiar organizing tactic, but a difficult tool for advocates of children. In order to boycott, you must have something to boycott; economic boycotts work, for example, because businesses need consumers to buy their products. . . . A boycott that utilizes children as the prized commodity may victimize the children by keeping them out of much needed services.

Consequently, we need to be especially careful in our use of the boycott. But, despite these warnings, consider the boycott as one of your potential tactics. Sometimes, a short boycott (one week, perhaps) can prove so embarrassing to the bureaucracy that you will win your objectives.

Aside from using the boycott as a way of gaining concessions, the boycott helps to publicize your needs and concerns. The boycott can be used to focus attention on a particular service agency. The opposite of boycott is a work-in or persistent demands for service. Parents, for example, refuse to leave a service agency until their children are served. This constitutes a reverse boycott.

Legal Action

Legal action includes: law suits; legal memoranda; legal rights booklets; civil rights statements; legal representation in fair hearings and other negotiations; and legal advice.

Purpose

Law has been a favorite strategy of nearly every social change movement in America. It is an indispensable tool for organizers.

Lawyers can offer many services other than as counsel in a court case. They play a critical role in the education of parent groups, consumers, and organizers. Whenever you organize around a human service issue, you should have working knowledge of the laws and rights. You can organize teach-ins on legal issues or you can develop organizing materials such as a legal rights manual or a legally based bill of rights for children.

Negotiation

Fair hearings; meetings with bureaucracies; individual negotiations; contract bargaining.

Purpose

In every type of organizing effort there will be many times when confrontation is not needed, when you can negotiate for the concessions you desire.

If the planners, teachers, social workers, administrators and psychologists show an interest in changing policies and meeting the needs of all children, negotiation may be your best tactic.

Even if you meet resistance, negotiation should be your first step in a series of actions; you can use the negotiations as a way of finding out where the bureaucracy stands.

You can use negotiations to achieve some of your goals while using other tactics (e.g., demands, legal actions, demonstrations, model programs, and lobbying) to meet other goals.

Working with Groups

Developing a group of advocates who act together but also provide resources to sustain each other is the building block of the child advocacy movement. Individuals can provide leadership and inspiration to others. Yet they need and must develop organizations that add clout to individual efforts, and that sustain action over a long time period.

Working with groups of people can be frustrating and time consuming. The child advocate can facilitate the effectiveness of the group by becoming more aware of roles that people play in groups and of useful techniques and processes.

Too bad there's not a simple recipe to create a cohesive group or a powerful advocate organization. Like advocacy itself, developing effective groups is an ongoing process. Excellent resources are available.[5] Some advocate groups ask outside trainers or consultants to help them work through problems in their groups' functioning so the primary tasks of the organization get accomplished.

Some important ingredients for effective functioning of advocacy groups have been identified by Designs for Change.[6]

With such a strong strain of individualism in American history and values, working with groups often feels frustrating and fruitless. Yet, until child advocates and children and parents learn to pull together in organizations and coalitions, very little will be changed for children in America.

INGREDIENTS OF EFFECTIVE ADVOCACY GROUPS

Take a good look at your group and rate its effectiveness by placing an X along the line ranging from Strong to Weak.

Leaders Work Together

Strong————————————————————— Weak

Group is not dominated by one person or faction with a specific interest. People with leadership and initiative work together in group.	Group is dominated by one person or faction. People with leadership and initiative don't stay with group.

A Focus Is Maintained

Strong_____ Weak

A program focus guides the group and they work persistently on that focus, repeatedly confronting the same people and issues.

Group jumps from one focus to another. Doesn't follow through over a long period on one issue.

Emotional Support Shared

Strong_____ Weak

Strong emotional ties exist around working for everyone's child. Available to each other when needed for information, support and reinforcement.

Much internal backbiting and manipulation. People have hidden agendas for participation. No feeling of unified purpose or emotional support.

Use Resource Networks and Coalitions

Strong_____ Weak

Group makes positive use of resource networks and coalitions.

Group works entirely on its own. Doesn't communicate with or make allies with others with common interests.

Dramatize Issues

Strong_____ Weak

Group dramatically brings issues to public attention using media and other techniques.

Group does nothing to publicize or communicate its views.

Complete Tasks

Strong———————————————— Weak

Members follow through on tasks. Can pull loose ends together and carry an assignment through to completion, even when it is not all spelled out.

Plans are made but not followed through. Responsibilities are confused.

High Level of Voluntary Participation

Strong———————————————— Weak

Group maintains a high level of voluntary participation and commitment.

A few do all the work. Volunteers drop out when paid staff is hired.

Learning from Painful Disagreements

Strong———————————————— Weak

Emerge from internal disagreements with understanding about how these issues will be dealt with better in the future. Learn from painful disagreements.

Internal disagreements destroy group. Problems swept under the rug without being resolved. Issues fester but are never resolved.

Skills of Members

Strong———————————————— Weak

Members have a high degree of acquired skill and expertise. Members share skills and knowledge with each other. High skill level contributes to credibility.

Members have low levels of expertise and downplay their importance. Members are defensive about skills they lack. Members who have skills and expertise are reluctant to share them.

Negotiating

Negotiating with people in power is an essential skill for advocates. An important part of any action plan is negotiating with officials. Some may be valuable allies. But others may be evasive or difficult to deal with. You must expect both kinds.

After a group has decided on the problems that need to be solved and changes that need to be made to meet its children's needs, demands (or requests) must be presented to the official who has the power to solve the problem. At this point, you must anticipate from officials responses that may be excuses for inaction.

The following list of possible responses that evade the issue or divert advocates from pressing their problems to a solution could be used as preparation for a meeting with officials.

We're the experts. "We know best and must make these decisions. You do not understand all the complex issues involved." Advocates must continually assert that they do know children's needs. Officials are paid by us to serve the needs of the children and the community.

Denial of the problem. "That is not a real problem. Do you have any proof?" Perhaps officials are not aware of the problems and the advocate group is serving an important role by informing them. Advocates should come to the meeting with evidence. (It should be documented, if possible. Firsthand reports are best.)

The exception. "The examples you cite are exceptions. It may be happening to just a few children; it certainly isn't widespread." Advocates should point out that each child is important and should ask the officials to prove the problem is not widespread. Put the burden of proof on the official. That is where it belongs, especially since advocates may not have access to all records.

Blaming the victim. "With this type of child, we really can't do that much." Blaming the child rather than the system, which itself may be structured to create problems, is a common way to avoid facing real problems. For example, a school is set up to serve the children of the community, and school officials are paid to design a school environment that meets the needs of all children.

Blaming the parents. "We know it's a problem, but those parents don't seem to care about their own children." Do not accept this attempt to evade the issue by shifting blame to parents. Hold officials accountable for what happens at agencies or institutions that they control. Advocates must not allow parents to be labeled "bad parents" because of their overwhelming problems or inadequate avenues of communication. An example is labeling parents of Spanish-speaking children as uneducated and uninterested in school when all school meetings are in English and school officials such as the principal and counselor can't speak Spanish.

Delaying. "Yes, I know the problem exists, but we need time to figure out the best thing to do." Ask specifically what is being done to solve the problems. Ask for their plans in writing with a timetable and the names of people responsible for implementing the plan.

Passing the buck. "Yes, that is a problem, but I can't do anything because my hands are tied (by policy, contracts, higher officials in the administration, the computer system)." Ask to see copies in writing of the policy, contracts, or memos that excuse the official from acting. If the official, in fact, is not accountable, then appeal over his head to the official who is responsible.

An unimportant problem. "Yes, it may be a problem but there are so many more pressing issues at this agency or institution." Do not be sidetracked. You believe the problem is important and should be dealt with because it affects children directly.

We're not so bad. "Yes, it's a problem in many places, but we're not doing any worse than others." Just because children in other agencies or institutions are not getting a quality service, these officials are not excused from doing their job properly. The standard for performance should be the needs of the children in your community, not the incompetence of officials.

Further study. "This problem needs further study and research before we can act wisely." Ask what can be done now to help the children who are suffering until the research is completed. (Also ask who is doing the study. Ask for the timetable for the research and plans for implementation.)

No money. "Yes, that's needed but we are short of funds and are facing budget cuts already." Lack of funds is a convenient excuse. Dig deeper to the issue of priorities. It may mean, "We do not want to spend money on what you want." Press the importance of what you see as priorities, which may mean cutting out an outdated program or position. But also raise the issue of getting more money for our children if the money pot is too small in the first place. If children are the most valuable resource for our country's future, local, state and federal governments need to fund public services adequately.

Negotiating skills can be sharpened in training workshops and by role playing in action-planning sessions. However, the best way to develop negotiating skills is to *do it*. Afterward, evaluate your strong and weak points, and you are sure to do it better the next time.

The skills of fact finding, planning action, negotiating and working with groups have been separated for the sake of discussion. However, in real-life situations, skills are often unconsciously developed and utilized to solve problems and are inextricably bound together. Planning and doing the constant fact finding as preparation for a negotiation situation usually involves working with groups, and the negotiation session often provides more facts that are needed to plan future steps.

Use facts as a basis for action and use action to uncover more facts. Some vital information can only be uncovered after taking action first.

Advocates should make a tentative plan of action but expect to keep uncovering more information with each step of the action plans. That is why it is so important to report back to the total group after taking an action.

This brief discussion of the basic skills that advocates develop as they assert the rights and needs of children is closely linked to the questions discussed in the next chapters: how do I use my role or roles as parent, staff person, or citizen to frame and add clout to my advocate role?

Notes

1. Excerpts from "What to Look for in Your Child's School" by Arlene Silberman is found in *The Open Classroom Reader* by Charles Silberman, Vintage, 1973. The article was originally printed in *The Ladies Home Journal,* Feb. 1971, pp. 39, 40, 48.

2. A list of national organizations that child advocates can turn to for research information are in chapter Nine.

3. Reports on children in jails, health care, schools, adoption and day care are available from the Children's Defense Fund. See chapter Nine.

4. This section has been adapted from chapter Two of *Parents Organizing to Improve Schools*, which I wrote for the National Committee for Citizens in Education, Suite 410, Wilde Lake Village Green, Columbia, Md., 21044.

5. See *Developing Leadership for Parent and Citizen Groups,* National Committee for Citizens in Education.

6. Designs for Change is a Chicago-based research-consulting group that has done careful analysis based upon firsthand observation of advocacy groups around the country. They have identified critical characteristics that groups need to work toward. This chart has been adapted from materials developed by Don Moore and Ularsee Manor as part of the school advocacy study. Designs for Change, 220 S. State St., Suite 1616, Chicago, Ill. 60604.

CHAPTER FIVE

STAFF PERSONS AS ADVOCATES

"**D**on't depend on lawyers to carry the ball in child advocacy. You are the most important advocates for many children." This is advice from a lawyer to teachers, social workers, child-care workers, and mental health counselors. The lawyer's role is very limited and is dependent on the professionals who work directly with children in schools, clinics, community agencies, and playgrounds. The staff persons in human service professions are in the best positions to know what children need, to recognize violations of rights, and to monitor the implementation of rights and services. Lawyers need you even more than you need them.

Human Service Workers Are Key

Professionals like teachers, child-care workers, nurses, doctors, mental health specialists, and social workers are in key positions to be advocates for children. Being paid to work and provide services to children and families, a staff person can act as mediator, negotiator, spokesperson, that is, as an advocate for the child when the system is not responding to the child's needs.

Direct service workers like teachers and child-care workers know the child intimately because of daily contact and interaction with the child. Next to the parent, he or she is often the most important adult in the child's life and the person who knows what the child needs.

Other professionals like doctors, social workers, and mental health specialists may not have daily contact with the child but are the persons who deliver services to the child and family. As the bridge between the child and the system, the professional staff person is in a strategic spot to see that quality services are delivered.

Stepping Into the Advocate Role

Staff persons spend most of their time in the role of provider of services—education, health, mental health, legal and social services. But when the system (agency, institution) is not responding to the child's needs, the human service professional temporarily *steps into the role of advocate*—to speak out for the child's interests, to mediate between the child and the system, and hopefully to negotiate a favorable resolution.

For example, a first-grade teacher may detect that a child needs glasses and know that the child is entitled to a free eye examination and glasses because of the family's income. The teacher steps into the role of advocate as she takes the initiative and follows up on a series of steps needed to get the glasses.

Examining Your Role

A beginning point for more effective advocacy by the staff person is role analysis. Namely, to ask oneself:

What power do I have in my role as staff person?

What are the limitations inherent in my role? (The chart on page 109 provides a format for role analysis by the individual or by a group of staff persons.)

What have I already done as an advocate—acting on behalf of children?

What are some issues in my present job situation that need attention and change?

With whom do I need to join forces to get those conditions, problems, and policies changed?

What specific problem is the best one to begin working on?

What are my strengths to build on and develop?

How can I build upon my strengths rather than bemoan my weaknesses?

Do I enable children to become their own advocates?

How can I support the parents' role as advocate?

Sources of Power

Staff persons functioning as child advocates must be aware of both the *power* inherent in their position and the *limitations* inherent in their role. The primary source of power is their understanding of the child and the child's needs gathered from hours of interaction and observation.

Because of their training and their knowledge of the agency (institution or system), the staff persons can seek out the assistance needed. The staff person as advocate is not there, in most cases, to replace the parents but rather to support and obtain resources for the child and family.

Since staff persons in an agency or institution are not permanent parent substitutes but rather supplements to the parent, they can usually avoid the emotional overload and some of the areas of potential conflict in the parent-child roles. The staff person is usually paid to do a job for eight hours. It is not a twenty-four hour, lifelong role. Thus, there are regular opportunities for relief and replenishing energy and emotional resources.

Staff persons, especially teachers, have professional organizations or unions that can provide support—and sometimes power and clout.

Staff can also use the legal rights of children and youth that have been established in the courts and legislation as a source of leverage and power. For example, look at the implications of the Education for All Handicapped Children Act (P.L. 94-142) for staff members in schools and clinics. Before the law was passed, a teacher or a counselor or mental health worker could identify a child needing special services and get the child tested by the school psychologist or mental health clinic. A comprehensive program could be drawn up. But when it was presented to the principal or even to the superintendent of schools, the response was often, "That's an excellent program and the child certainly does need help. I wish we could provide it, but we're not able to now. Maybe in a couple of years when we have more money for additional staff and services." The only recourse then for the teacher or counselor was to return to the classroom or clinic in frustration and despair and wait for the "next year" that seldom came.

With the passage of the law, the teacher, counselor, mental health worker, and psychologist have new leverage to get help for children with special needs. Now staff members attend the case conference that develops the Individualized Education Plan and they can persist until an appropriate placement is made. The law is now there in many situations to be used on behalf of children. The law is a source of power for staff persons who know the rights of the child, parent, and staff person and who then skillfully and persistently use the law for leverage in the system.

Limitations

The agency or institution may place restrictions and expectations on the staff that limit their flexibility and effectiveness. As one mental health counselor noted, agency policy that required all children and families to come to the mental health center rather than allowing the counselor to work both in and out of the office restricted her effectiveness. Some institutions have a tradition of holding case conferences with "professionals only" and excluding the direct service worker like the child-care worker, mental health aide, or classroom aide from critical decisions about the child.

Another limitation on staff persons is that their job security and status may be jeopardized in some advocacy situations. Therefore, it is very important for the professional to know both the formal and informal power structure and decision-making processes within the agency and the system. Membership in a professional organization or union can often provide some protection. Or the staff person can develop links with parent and citizen groups who can use the information available to "paid insiders" for their activity as volunteer "outside" consumers. The professional should also be aware of the wide variety of advocacy strategies that can resolve a problem before it becomes a confrontation or adversarial situation.[1]

Another limitation on staff persons is "burn out." Large bureaucracies often have self-serving forces that grind down the well-meaning worker. The experience of this young teacher illustrates just one situation that a staff person may face.

> The young man is in his senior year of college. He likes working with people. He wants to help children. Perhaps he should try teaching, his friends suggest. He takes an examination at the Board of Education. He meets a principal who offers him a job in his school. But when he arrives at that school in September, he finds out that headquarters had not marked his exam and that therefore he had no file number. He is told that he cannot start working without a file number. He must take an emergency examination, which will be marked immediately. He does all these things, and this time he is assigned to an entirely different school, late in the term, where no one knows him and, more important, where he knows no one either. (Meanwhile, of course, in his former school a class has gone uncovered and he is sorely missed.)

The new principal seems glad to see him. She assigns him to Class 5-5. She doesn't tell him that this is one of the most "difficult" classes in the school and that none of her regular teachers would accept that assignment. She wishes him luck and leaves him with the children. He tries. How hard he tries! His classroom is chaotic. The workbooks have not arrived so the children have to copy everything off the board. He is constantly interrupted by messages from the office or announcements over the loudspeaker. He cannot get the children to sit still. He attends his first staff meeting, hoping that he will learn something about the school, hoping he will find out where to go for help. But all they discuss are fire-drill regulations and lunchroom procedures. He learns to keep his classroom door closed so the rest of the school won't hear the shouting. Four weeks after he has started, the principal comes by to congratulate him for the good job he is doing. She has heard no noise, so she tells him he is doing well. Is that all she wanted? Rather grimly he decides, "If I can't teach them, at least I can keep them quiet." And the rest of the year he learns how to control his class. At the end of the term, his probationary report is marked "Satisfactory," and he breathes a sigh of relief. "Maybe," he decides, "that is all we can do for those children."

Who is the villain in that story? The young man, the principal, or the system? Was the principal herself once like that young man, and also defeated and reshaped by the system?[2]

Providing direct services to children and families can be emotionally and physically exhausting. It often takes extra time and energy to be an advocate or to equip the child or the parents to be advocates for themselves. Working with people, unlike working with machines or paper, is endlessly complex. The staff person must know how to clarify goals and set some limits. The professional also needs to seek out allies and resources for new energy. Staff meetings, conferences, and continuing education courses can be the medium for revitalization. Advocates in an agency or institution may want to set up a support group to provide a forum for airing frustrations and sharing successes and new ideas.[3]

And finally, staff persons must keep their role clear. The staff person is *not* the policymaker, the administrator, the parent, or the child. Although the grass often looks greener under someone else's feet, the staff person must know who he/she is and is *not*.

Sample Role Analysis for the Advocate

Examining one's powers and limitations in a specific role is one way to clarify one's role and set realistic expectations. A direct service worker like a child-care worker or teacher may identify these powers and limitations.

POWER inherent in my role as a _____

1. I have direct contact with children.

2. I know children's needs.

3. I care about each child.

4. I know how the agency or system functions—at least better than the child and many parents.

5. I belong to a professional association or union for job security and protection.

6. I can give vital information to parent groups or independent advocacy groups.

LIMITATIONS inherent in my role as a _____

1. I am tied down by responsibilities of job—time, job description, accountability. I'm just struggling to survive.

2. I don't have real power in the system—others make policy and set priorities.

3. I risk being fired if I "rock the boat."

4. I will not be promoted if I "make trouble."

5. I am at the mercy of bureaucratic procedures and pressures to conform.

6. I don't have the power and freedom that parents, policymakers, or lawyers have.

7. I can use my role as citizen, taxpayer, voter, in addition to professional role.	7. I am dependent upon the cooperation and expertise of others. 8. I feel "burned out" and frustrated.

The Professional Child Advocate

Up to this point, professionals referred to have been the staff persons in agencies and institutions that provide direct services to children and families. A new specialized profession is emerging—that of the professional child advocate whose job is to intervene on behalf of children in a specific system or institution. For example, some parent and citizen organizations employ staff persons who work as advocates for children and families in the school system and/or the juvenile justice system. Some hospitals employ a patient advocate who looks out for the child's best interests in the hospital. Lawyers have been appointed by the courts to represent the interests of the child in divorce and placement cases.

The distinguishing features of the professional advocate's role is that the person is hired to represent, look out for, and guarantee that the child's needs are met by the institution or system. These interests may be different from the interests of the staffs, the parents, or the bureaucratic forces in the system itself.

Some of the difficult questions are, Who will pay the salary of and hire the professional child advocate? How can the advocate's independence be preserved so that the child's interests, not the institution's interests, are paramount? Should the advocate be accountable to a person or group inside or outside the institution?

Long-term, effective advocacy on behalf of the children is long overdue, but is developing. Continued growth of the child advocacy movement will depend upon the staff people who work daily with children. No advocacy system initiated by the government or by private institutions will be successful unless the people working directly with children have the under-standing, skills, and organizational supports to exercise their advocacy roles.

Marian Wright Edelman
Professional Advocate for Children

Marian Wright Edelman has been active in civil rights and public interest affairs since her graduation from Yale Law School in 1963. She started and directed the NAACP Legal Defense and Education Fund Office in Jackson, Mississippi from 1964-1968. During this period, she was deeply involved in numerous school desegregation cases and served on the Board of the Child Development Group of Mississippi, one of the largest Head Start programs in the country with over 100 centers in mostly rural, poor communities throughout the state.

In 1968, Mrs. Edelman founded the Washington Research Project, which became the Children's Defense Fund in 1973, and has served as director since its inception. CDF has been active in a wide range of children and family issues. It has published numerous reports on children out of school, health care, social services, child welfare and adoption. CDF has been a leader in defending and expanding the rights of children through the courts—blocking the placement of Louisiana children in out-of-state Texas institutions, guaranteeing special education rights in Mississippi, and in represent-ing systematically the interests of children and families before federal administrative agencies. In addition, CDF has actively promoted the need for expanded quality child care and other services for children, and the need to preserve a strong, federal, civil rights capability.

In recent years, Mrs. Edelman traveled to Hanoi as a member of the President's Commission on MIAs and undertook a two-week, privately sponsored mission to South Africa.

Notes

1. See chapter Four above.

2. Ellen Lurie, *How to Change the Schools,* Random House, pp. 81-82.

3. See John Westman's book, *Child Advocacy* (Free Press, Macmillan, 1979), which has five chapters on advocacy issues that professionals find in school, the legal system, social services, health care, and mental health. It provides an excellent detailed discussion with a comprehensive bibliography. Another pertinent resource is *Child Advocacy Within the System* (Syracuse University Press, 1977) by Paul, Neufeld, and Pelosi.

CHAPTER SIX

PARENTS AS ADVOCATES

A few weeks ago my handicapped child, who is an epileptic, fell down. He had a big blow in his eye, the pain was terrible. I had to call somebody to lend me money to bring him to the hospital. After he stayed there an hour and a half crying, because my child was in such terrible pains, the hospital told me there was no doctor to see me, only assistants, attendants . . . so I really was crying on the way—I had to walk eight more blocks to bring him to another hospital. And in that other hospital they said we don't have a specialist in the eyes at this hour because poor people cannot get sick after 5:30 on Saturdays and Sundays in this city. . . . (A parent testifying before U.S. Senate, 1971.)[1]

Parents are the advocates for their children—negotiating with the school system, health system, economic system, law enforcement system—even with the TV industry to secure proper care for their children's development. Hardly a week goes by where a parent doesn't need to act on behalf of a son or daughter. Yet for many parents, it is a frustrating and lonely job. For the single parent, the responsibilities of providing basic necessities plus nurture are especially heavy. One out of every six American children lives with a single parent. For the parents of 17 million children

113

who survive at a poverty level, the barriers seem insurmountable. As one mother sadly relates:

> My children have troubles. In school they tell them they need to have their eyes looked at, and their teeth. They say I'm not feeding them the right food. . . . I'm trying, I am. I'm going to do it; I'm going to get the children looked at someplace, in a hospital, and buy them the clothes they need. All I lack is the *money*, then I can go and do those things they tell you to do: take the taxis, and visit the teachers, go to the hospital, and demand your rights at the welfare office, and all that. (A mother to Robert Coles in *Children of Crisis,* 1967.)

Blaming the Parents

Despite the efforts of most parents to secure the best for their children, parents are often blamed for their children's

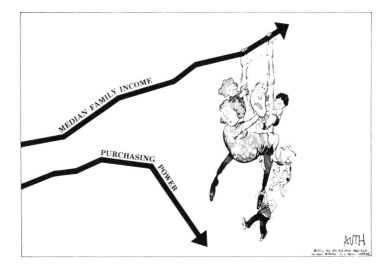

failures and problems. "Blaming the parent" is a scapegoating technique of many people in power—politicians, teachers, psychologists, police.[2] Yet numerous research studies question the assumption that parents are the most powerful influence on a child's development and therefore should be blamed (or praised) for the child's failures (or successes).[3]

A more fruitful approach is to see the parent as a primary but not the only powerful influence on the child's development. The parent, *along with* teachers, peers, TV, grandparents, pets, hobbies, and the neighborhood, shapes the child's development.

The Carnegie Council on Children asserts:

> . . . we must address ourselves less to the criticism and reform of parents themselves than to the criticism and reform of the institutions that sap their self-esteem and power. . . . The problem is not so much to re-educate parents but to make available help they need and to give them enough *power* so that they can be effective advocates with and coordinators of the other forces that are bringing up their children.[4]

Parents' Rights—A Basis for Advocacy

Parents' rights are a beginning point for getting that power, for more effective advocacy by parents. A right established by law can reinforce the position of parents who are trying to secure the best for their child. Instead of begging the hospital to care for her son, the mother quoted above would have been in a much more powerful position had she been able to say: "My son has a right to be given emergency medical treatment. I demand that you serve him or I will call an advocate at the legal aid office." Unfortunately, clear-cut rights to medical care for children and procedures to enforce the rights are not written into the law to date.

Parents' rights that can be the basis for advocacy do exist in a few areas. Let's look briefly at some of the specific rights of parents in public schools—the second home where most children spend 900 hours a year for twelve or more years of their childhood.[5]

Right to Inspect School Records

Sharon's parents could not understand why their daughter was not accepted into nursing school, when her high school grades were good.[6]

Checking with high school officials, they went over her cumulative school records. Here they found that one teacher had written that Sharon had, "a history of trouble-making" in class. She had, indeed, had a series of personality clashes with that teacher, though her academic work in the class had been satisfactory.

Working with the school administration, her parents had the negative notation removed from the records, and Sharon was subsequently admitted to the nursing school of her choice.

A parent group in New York City accidentally discovered that one child's records contained, for the information of the next year's teacher, this notation:

> "A real sickie—absent, truant, stubborn and very dull . . . can barely read. Have fun!"

These are only two examples of damaging materials kept in school records that led to a federal law commonly called the Buckley Amendment passed in August 1974. The law was the first such legislation to affect all parents in the United States. It guarantees them the right to:

1. Inspect their children's school records.
2. Challenge false, misleading material and have it removed from the records.
3. Be informed and have the right to withhold consent if the record is to be released to persons or agencies outside the school.

This last provision prevents release of the material to the

FBI, police, prospective employers, colleges, researchers or others without the parents' written permisson.

The new law, the Family Educational Rights and Privacy Act (Public Law 93-380), not only establishes parents' rights to see their children's school records, but also requires each school district to draw up a set of guidelines detailing how records will be handled, how long they will be kept, and how students' rights of privacy will be protected.

Parents are also entitled to copies of the records. School districts provide the first copy free. Each district must have written guidelines on conditions under which the records may be examined, providing safeguards, such as keeping track of who has had access to the material.

Parents who feel they may have trouble understanding the records may ask for explanations, and for the right to have another person with them while they examine the material.

It is not generally known that the cumulative record or "packet," which follows a child from grade to grade, and school to school, may contain a teacher's subjective opinions, psychological evaluations of which the parents know nothing, and personal family data.

The complete school records may include information on academic progress and test results; health examinations; attendance record; discipline problems, and family background. Parents should make sure they are shown the entire record.

Any school district that fails to comply with the law faces the loss of federal funds. Parents who feel their local school districts are not complying can file complaints with the U. S. Department of Health, Education and Welfare, 330 Independence Avenue, S.W., Washington, D. C., 20201.

Right to a Fair Hearing

Nine-year-old Larry is a lucky boy.

It might not have seemed so last winter, when the principal at his school ordered him transferred to a special disciplinary school. The second institution was known as a dumping ground for the violent, disturbed element in the public schools. A slight, shy boy like Larry would have been terrorized and possibly physically harmed there.

He was lucky on two counts. One, his parents cared enough (and knew enough) to look into his options. Two, he lived in one of the school districts where the courts had ordered hearings to be held before such transfers could be made.

At Larry's hearing, before the principal and an impartial school district official, Larry admitted he had been disrupting the class. He explained that he felt the teacher had disciplined him unfairly at the beginning of the year, and he was getting back at her.

It was agreed that he was basically a good student and would certainly not be helped in a disciplinary school. He promised to straighten out, his parents promised to see that he did, and the principal agreed to retain him in the school.

This is one example of a situation in which parents and children should be granted fair hearings. Law and policy vary among school districts. In some, the courts have established clear guidelines,[7] while in other districts no consistent procedures are followed and parents have no specific law to use as the basis for their action.

In the case of suspensions, the U.S. Supreme Court has established specific due process procedures (*Goss* v. *Lopez*)[8] for suspension of ten days or less. The student must be given fair notice of the charges against him and an opportunity to explain his side of the story.

In suspensions of more than ten days and cases of expulsion, more formal procedures and hearings are in order, although the U.S. Supreme Court has set no clear guidelines. Formal hearings usually include:

1. An impartial hearing officer, *not* a school representative personally involved in the case.
2. The right to bring counsel—a lawyer, parent advocate, minister or other person.
3. The right to cross-examine witnesses.
4. The right to present evidence.

5. The right to a written decision.
6. The right to appeal the decision in the courts, if necessary.

The parents should be given ample notice of the hearing, so that they can arrange to attend.

The issue here is a major one. Decisions are made affecting the child's whole future. Too often they are made without thorough consultation with the parent, and with no provision for the parent to appeal them. Hearings are one way to insure parental involvement in working out solutions to problems a child is having in school.

In addition to the rights of hearing and appeal, parents should have the right to a grievance procedure for all complaints. (Note that I said *should* rather than *do*. Such procedures exist in only a few local school districts.)

Suggested elements of a grievance procedure:

1. A hearing with the local school official, probably the principal, and with an impartial person when needed.
2. An appeals procedure, leading ultimately to the courts, if necessary.
3. Reasonable time limits—for example, an appointment within five school days, a written decision after three days, an appeal to a higher level within ten days.
4. A written decision given to the parent either in person or by mail.
5. Permission for the parent to be accompanied by a parent advocate, whether a lawyer, friend, or relative.
6. Details of the procedure printed in a parent handbook, to be given personally or mailed to every parent at the beginning of the school year.

There is no reason why a grievance procedure, an integral part of all good teachers' contracts, should be denied to the parents who pay teachers' salaries.

Right to Education for All Handicapped Children

Mary Ellen suffered brain damage at birth. Her development was severely delayed. At the age of five she was just beginning to feed herself and to walk. She had four brothers and sisters and her father earned a moderate income.

The family wanted to keep the child at home rather than place her in an institution, but the stresses on the family were severe. The public school officials in their community said they did not have a classroom situation for a child as seriously handicapped as Mary Ellen. So the family found a private school for handicapped children which cost them $2,500 per year since 1970. The costs of a college education for the other four siblings and the anticipated twelve-year drain on their family resources for private school for Mary Ellen were weighing heavily on the family when they heard that Congress had passed new legislation in 1975 called Education for All Handicapped Children Act, Public Law 94-142.

Mary Ellen's parents contacted the local association of parents of handicapped children. With their assistance and with steady persistent lobbying and negotiating with school officials during the next year and a half, they were able to get Mary Ellen placed in a newly established classroom for severely handicapped children at the local school by September 1978.

The new federal law had a profound effect on Mary Ellen's family. It gave them a legal basis to work from in their negotiations with schools. The law says children can no longer be turned away from the public schools because of the type or severity of their handicap. The public schools must provide an education for all handicapped children, either within the public school system or else payment for placement in a private setting if no public school program is appropriate.

In addition, the law (94-142) calls for an "appropriate" placement that is agreed upon by the parents, the child, if he/she is able, and the school personnel—like teacher, counselor, and principal. Thorough testing of the child by school psychologists and any necessary outside specialists is an obvious prior step in the process. The placement decision is spelled out in an IEP (Individualized Educational Program) that must be evaluated at least once a year.

Full due process procedures are spelled out in the federal law (PL 94-142) if the parents and school officials cannot agree on a placement and IEP. Fair hearing and appeal procedures outlined above are spelled out in PL 94-142, along with the parents' rights to inspect the child's records.

This federal law gives parents of handicapped children in every state a powerful lever to secure a proper education for their child. The power is there in the law but it will still take persistent efforts by parents and advocacy organizations to translate the words on paper into excellent educational programs for all handicapped children.

Parent Organizations—Needed for Long-term Systems Change

Legal rights are one source of support for the parent. Another support are parent organizations whereby the individual can work with, lean upon, and learn from other parents. Feeling alone and powerless, the individual needs a group—and better yet—a permanent organization that exists to advocate the children's best interests.

Organizations are the basis of power in the highly bureaucratic, technological society in which we live. "Organize or perish" was the dictum for working people in the early 20th century. "Organize or perish" is now the dictum for consumers in the last quarter of the 20th century. Parents as advocates for their children must develop parent organizations for sustained advocacy that forces big systems to be more responsible to children.[10]

There is increasing evidence that parent-initiated and controlled organizations are most effective for long-term advocacy.[11] Even though they require precious time, sweat, and dollars and are difficult to organize and sustain over the years, self-initiated, independent organizations are needed not only for the problems actually solved, but also for the monitoring of institutionally mandated and controlled parent groups, and as a resource for professionals in the system who need help from parents who are not employed or controlled by the system.

Children's Rights:

According to the Education for All Handicapped Children Act and its proposed regulations handicapped children have the right to:

1. a Free and Appropriate Public Education (FAPE) if they are between the ages of three and eighteen by September 1, 1978 and if three and twenty-one by September 1, 1980.

2. the same variety of programs and services that children without handicaps enjoy, including nonacademic subjects and extracurricular activities.

3. placement in the least restrictive learning environment, as much as possible with non-handicapped children and whenever possible at the same school they would go to if not handicapped.

4. the availability of a number of alternative learning settings if attending a local public school is not possible.

5. priority use of supplemental federal funds for those not now being served at all.

6. appointment of a person to act as parent, to be the child's advocate and to participate in evaluation and program meetings with the school if natural parents are unavailable or if the child is a ward of the state.

7. participation in the writing of their own Individual Educational Program (IEP) "where appropriate."

8. placement outside the local school district in another public school or a private school at the state's expense if local schools do not have an appropriate program.

9. testing for purposes of evaluation and placement that is free of racial or cultural discrimination.

10. an annual review of placement based on IEP and at least an annual review of that program before each school year begins.

11. remain in present placement during any administrative or judicial proceeding or the right to attend a public school if the complaint involves an application for admission to public school.

12. privacy and confidentiality of all personal records.

Parents' Rights:

According to the Education For All Handicapped Children Act and its proposed regulations, as parents of handicapped children, you have the right to:

1. participate in the annual planning meetings for child's Individual Educational Program (IEP) and annual evaluation.

2. agree to a time and place for those meetings (always held before the beginning of the affected school year).

3. instruct the local school agency to hold those meetings in your primary language (or make special arrangements for your handicap, if any, including deafness) so that you can understand the proceedings.

4. give your consent before an evaluation is conducted.

5. give voluntary written consent to any activities proposed for your child.

6. seek an independent evaluation of your child at public expense if you find the school's evaluation inappropriate. (The school may request a hearing to decide the appropriateness of its evaluation. If the ruling is in the school's favor, you still have the right to submit an independent evaluation which must be considered but which is then conducted at your expense.)

7. have written notice of any proposed change in identification, evaluation or placement of your child or the school's refusal to change any of those.

8. attend and comment at the annual public hearings held prior to adoption of state program plans. (Hearings must be publicized in advance.)

9. receive a full explanation of procedural safeguards and a description of any proposed action regarding your child and their basis.

10. see, review and, if necessary, challenge your child's record in accordance with the Family Educational Rights and Privacy Act of 1974.

11. request a hearing on any proposal to initiate or change the identification, evaluation or placement of your child, or the agency's refusal to do so within forty-five days of your request.

12. request a copy of information from your child's record before it is destroyed in compliance with the law, five years after its usefulness ends.[9]

The distinguishing features of the new brand of parent advocacy groups that are evolving are:

1. the focus on specific actions that will change systems (rather than on just fund raising and social activities);
2. the requirement that parents control the organization (rather than control by professionals or administrators employed by the system);
3. the understanding that rights backed by the law are a basis for real, not just token, power.

Parent Advocate Service

"My son is being transferred to a disciplinary school. Can you help me?"

"They want to put Judy in a class with all retarded children—but her handicap is cerebral palsy. What can I do?"

"My son was struck and pushed against the wall by the gym teacher. Do I have any rights? I'm so angry I want to sue him."

"My child needs help. She's bright enough—but still can't read. Where can I get her tested by a good doctor or psychologist?"

Begun as a response to desperate calls for help from parents who want to help their children but don't know where to turn, a parent advocate service[12] evolves as a self-help effort of parents who have learned to negotiate the system and then volunteer to assist other parents.

Parent advocates are trained to provide assistance. They listen first, then give information about rights, policies, and programs. They discuss options, go with the parents to conferences, informal hearings, and even formal hearings with officials. They refer the parent to lawyers or other agencies when needed. Often the most important role of the parent advocate is giving support—so that the parent does not feel alone and powerless.

Most parents are in the best spot to be advocates for their children,[13] but in order to negotiate more effectively with the complex, bureaucratized systems that dominate their family's lives, parents need legal rights that they understand, organizations to provide support and significant systems change, and trained parent advocates to give specialized help with specific problems. Hopefully, parents will be one of the groups of consumers who organize in the last quarter of the 20th century and regain some power in the decision-making processes that shape their children's lives.

Notes

1. From *It's Time to Stand Up For Your Children: A Parents' Guide to Child Advocacy.* Children's Defense Fund. See also *America's Children 1976,* p. 59 (available from G. National Coalition for Children and Youth, 1910 K Street, N.W., Washington, D.C., 20006).

2. William Ryan, *Blaming the Victim,* Vintage, 1971.

3. See Arlene Skolnick's brief, well-written review of research on this issue in *Psychology Today,* February 1978, "The Myth of the Vulnerable Child."

4. Kenneth Keniston and The Carnegie Council on Children, *All Our Children: The American Family Under Pressure,* Harcourt Brace Jovanovich, New York, 1977, p. 23.

5. For a more detailed and comprehensive survey of parents' rights, see David Schimmel and Louis Fischer, *The Rights of Parents in the Education of Their Children,* 1977, published by the National Committee for Citizens in Education, Suite 410, Wilde Lake Village Green, Columbia, Maryland, 21044. See also Alan Sussman, *The Rights of Students,* 2nd edition, Avon/Discus and ACLU.

6. Some of this material on parents' rights is taken from an unpublished article that Catherine Green coauthored with me.

7. In Philadelphia, for example, the courts have ruled that a student cannot be transferred to a disciplinary school unless proper due process procedures have been followed.

8. *Goss* v. *Lopez,* 419 U.S. 565 (1972). See also *Suspensions and Due Process,* available from the Robert F. Kennedy Memorial (1035 30th Street, N.W., Washington, D.C., 20007).

9. *Network,* Feb. 1977, National Committee for Citizens in

Education. See also *94-142 and 504: Numbers that Add Up to Educational Rights for Handicapped Children,* published by the Children's Defense Fund, 1520 New Hampshire Avenue, N.W., Washington, D.C., 20036.

10. See Fernandez, "Empowering Parents," *The Urban Review,* vol. 11, no. 2, Summer 1979.

11. See the National Institute for Education study of parent and citizen involvement in schools by Don Davies, *Patterns of Citizen Participation in Educational Decision-making,* available from Institute for Responsible Education, 704 Commonwealth Avenue, Boston, Massachusetts, 02215.

12. Parents' Union for Public Schools in Philadelphia (401 N. Broad Street, Room 1006, Philadelphia, Pennsylvania, 19108) has developed a parent advocate service. See case of Vera Simon described in chapter Two. It shows how the parent advocate assisted a parent and student.

13. See, *It's Time to Stand Up for Your Children: A Parents' Guide to Child Advocacy,* Children's Defense Fund publication.

CHAPTER SEVEN

CHILDREN
AS ADVOCATES

Children can be advocates for themselves and for other children. A major goal for adult advocates is to empower and enable young people to secure the services they need from our institutions and systems.

Adults who are advocates for children will want to consider questions like, What are ways that I as an adult can encourage and enable children to be advocates for themselves? What kinds of supports and resources can adults provide? What kinds of skills and organizations do children need to develop as advocates? What can adults do to sensitize other adults to children's rights and needs?

The Adult's Role—Enabling and Responding

Sometimes children can be effective where adults meet roadblocks. In one such case, a letter-writing campaign by elementary school students was instrumental in getting the water fountains repaired on the school playground. The principal had filed requests for five months to the school district maintenance department with no results. The week following the children's letters to the maintenance supervisor,

White House proposes Youth Energy Patrols.
—News Item

district supervisor, and superintendent, the water fountains were fixed. The role of the principal in this case was to do all he could in his role as principal to use proper channels, and he took the extra step of encouraging the young people to act on their own behalf when adult measures had failed.

But advocacy by children can also be solely initiated by children. Then the adult's role is to respond appropriately to implement requests. In one such instance, Susan, a seven-year-old student came to her principal's office to request that milk be served at the end of the school day rather than ten in the morning because the children were then still full from breakfast and the lunch period began at 11:45. By 3:00 the children were hungry. The principal replied that it was a good idea but that he could not make a change for the whole school just because Susan wanted it. He also detailed all the administrative problems involved, including extra work for the kitchen staff. The principal assumed he had heard the end of it. Susan came back eight days later with a petition signed by every child in the school and a supportive note from the kitchen staff. All wanted milk served at the end of the school day. Surprised and impressed, he granted their request and implemented it.

Children Know, Care, and Act

Children as advocates need to combine the same qualities as adult advocates—knowing, caring and acting. The adult's role is to respect and nurture these characteristics.

Children do know—themselves, the system, and their rights. They do not need to know better than adults, which is the trap some critics fall into. The point is that children do know. The adult must first listen intently and only then develop ways to assist young people to broaden their knowledge base and to act effectively.

One sign of adult arrogance is the assumption that the adult knows what's best for the child—often without even consulting the child or teenager. Until recently, children were not consulted in critical life decisions such as whom they would prefer to live with in divorce and foster care disputes,[1] whether they had committed a crime and should be imprisoned,[2] or whether a young woman wanted to bear a child.[3]

Children are not only knowledgeable about themselves and their needs, they have insights and opinions about the institutions and agencies that have been set up to serve them. For example, in a survey of 10,000 Massachusetts fifth and sixth graders, Dr. Robert Sinclair[4] found that the students had some astute observations and strong feelings about how the system really worked. "Through the Eyes of Children" noted that the teachers of those students predicted that students would rate schools higher than the children actually did.

Powerfully specific and direct testimony about how the juvenile penal system actually works was presented by young people who had spent years in our prisons and training schools. The testimony was given at the Hearings on Incarcerated Children held by the Children's Express, a group of young people who have formed their own reporting service.[5] They held the hearings in Washington, D. C., as a way to draw public attention to the abuses in the juvenile "justice" system. Thus, in this unique instance, young people held public hearings to enable other young people to speak out about the abuse they had suffered and that will continue unless changes are made and enforced in the system. One teenager described her psychological trauma and despair while serving a fifty-day sentence in solitary confinement. Another young man described his experiences of being drugged repeatedly in violation of regulations and guidelines—1,100 units of thorazine in one day.

Adults provided assistance at multiple levels to enable the Children's Express to stage the public hearings that give other young people the opportunity to speak out about the system that had abused them behind closed doors. Financial and technical assistance plus consultation were essential contributions by adults.

Children and Their Rights

Children want to know their rights. The adult's role is to enable them to be aware of and understand their lawful rights. In one case, eight-year-old Jimmy questioned his Mom, "I thought you said a teacher was not supposed to hit children: Why is Mrs. Jones allowed to hit kids in our class with a ruler? I thought you said that was against the law."[6] Surprised at the sharp memory of her youngest son and at the alleged action of the new substitute that parents had helped find while the regular teacher was out on maternity leave, Jimmy's mother first asked him for more details on what was happening in the classroom. Jimmy had not been hit, but he was anxious and afraid that he might be. Jimmy's mother then reassured him that the law and the school district policy did prohibit physical punishment of children and that she would see what could be done. She was very careful not to jump to conclusions and not to undermine the teacher-child relationship. After contacting several other parents of children in that classroom and the school principal to get further information, she attended a meeting with the substitute, the principal, and several parents to resolve the problem. Several weeks later Jimmy commented, "Mom, Mrs. Jones has stopped using the ruler. I like our classroom better now, but I'll be glad when Mrs. Murray has her baby and comes back. How did you get Mrs. Jones to stop using the ruler?" Jimmy's mother briefly described the steps that she had taken and carefully noted that his knowledge of the rules on corporal punishment had been very important.

Assisting young people to be familiar with their legal rights is an essential role of the child advocate. How many young people have been intentionally and thoroughly informed of rights that they have in schools, in the streets, in the courts, and in the work place? In a few communities, a wallet-sized student's rights or juvenile's rights card is distributed. The Dayton (Ohio) Students' Rights Center has a slide-tape presentation on students' rights. Another valuable resource are the handbooks prepared by the American Civil Liberties Union, *The Rights of Young People* and *The Rights of Students.*

Some school districts have adopted a Student Bill of Rights and Responsibilities and distribute it each fall to students. Yet, only a few school districts interrelate the material studied in American history or American government with the rights of students. What better way to understand the Bill of Rights than to examine the Supreme Court's decision in the case of fifteen-year-old John Tinker and the court's guarantee of a student's First Amendment rights. John Tinker, his thirteen-year-old sister, Mary Beth, and sixteen-year-old Christopher Eckhardt were the plaintiffs in the case that went all the way to the Supreme Court and clearly established that school students have the right of free speech in school. They were suspended from school in 1965 for wearing black armbands in protest of the Vietnam War. The Des Moines, Iowa school authorities had gotten wind of the students' intention to wear black armbands and had quickly met to adopt a policy that students who refused to remove the black armbands would be suspended until they agreed to return to school without the armbands.

The Supreme Court ruled:

> . . . the action of the school authorities appears to have been based upon an urgent wish to avoid the controversy which might result from the expression, even by the silent symbol of armbands, of opposition to this Nation's part in the conflagration in Vietnam. It is revealing, in this respect, that the meeting at which the school principals decided to issue the contested regulation was called in response to a student's statement to the journalism teacher in one of the schools that he wanted to write an article on Vietnam and have it published in the school paper. (The student was dissuaded.)
>
> It is also relevant that the school authorities did not purport to prohibit the wearing of all symbols of political or controversial significance. The record shows that students in some of the schools wore buttons relating to national political campaigns, and some even wore the Iron Cross, traditionally a symbol of Nazism. The order prohibiting the wearing of armbands did not extend to these. Instead, a particular symbol—black armbands worn to exhibit opposition to this Nation's involvement in Vietnam—was singled out for prohibition. Clearly, the prohibition of expression of one particular opinion, at least without evidence that it is necessary to avoid material and substantial interference with schoolwork or discipline, is not constitutionally permissible.
>
> In our system, state-operated schools may not be enclaves of totalitarianism. School officials do not possess absolute authority over their students. Students in school as well as out of school are "persons" under our Constitution. They are possessed of fundamental rights which the State must respect, just as they themselves must respect their obligations to the State. In our system, students may not be confined to the expression of those sentiments that are officially approved. In the absence of a specific showing of constitutionally valid reasons to regulate their speech, students are entitled to freedom of expression of their views.[7]

The case of fifteen-year-old Gerald Gault that resulted in the famous 1967 decision by the U. S. Supreme Court is another case that interests and affects young people. The meaning of the Fourteenth Amendment's guarantee of due process procedures in the courts would be very clear to young people after studying the case. The Supreme Court decision describes the facts of the case and the issues at stake.[8]

Many young people are hungry for information on their rights and for schoolwork that is relevant to their lives. But often, experience is the best teacher. How many schools have a policy and structure that fosters a decision-making role for students? How many schools have a version of the school site council where students have significant representation and vote on basic policy in the school? How many schools have a clearly defined and written grievance procedure where a student can appeal decisions made by teachers, principals, and other students? Young people learn to exercise their rights and to be advocates for their needs through experience and practice. The school is the best place to begin. Schools, especially at the senior high level, need to be restructured to enable young people to have a significant role in the decision-making process.

Young people want to know, and they do care, despite being labeled apathetic, irresponsible, and self-centered. Many young people have a passionate yearning to help create a just, human society. But their frustrations, disappointments, and feelings that no one really listens to or respects them are very similar to the feelings that adult advocates have—the staff person who feels like a cog in the bureaucracy or the parent who is "just a parent."

Adult Advocates Provide Assistance

Staff people within the school who see themselves as advocates for children can help change the structure of decision-making within the school to include rather than exclude students. In some states and school districts, school site councils have been formed that have decision-making authority. The councils are composed of consumers (fifty percent of the membership being students and parents, and fifty percent representing staff and the administration).[9]

A National Coalition of Advocates for Students formed in 1978 to provide a communication network for advocate groups in local communities and to monitor legislation and litigation at the national level that affects students, especially around discipline issues.[10] It is, however, a coalition of advocacy groups that are adult-run.

The Youth Project [11] is a national fund-raising group that distributes resources to projects at the local level, some of which are controlled by young people. The work of the Youth Project touches that knotty problem of providing financial resources to youth organizations, some of which may not have the stability and "credibility" that make them a "good risk" for other foundations. Yet, lack of resources to pay for organizational necessities like telephones, paper, a bookkeeper, and an answering device is one common cause of organizational instability and failure.

Organizations of, by, and for Young People

High school students can be effective advocates for themselves. Student unions in some school districts work as advocates for students by influencing the school board and its contract negotiations, maintaining a hotline, serving as ombudsmen, and informing students of their rights and responsibilities. But in most school districts, student organizations are ineffective, poorly organized, controlled by the administration, and/or focused on social activities rather than on students' rights and policy decisions in the school.

Organizing and developing an effective student organization is even more difficult than maintaining a parent group. Some obstacles inherent in student life are:

—Competing interests and responsibilities like academic work, after school jobs, sports and social affairs.

—The relatively short time—four years—that a student is at the school creates a rapid turnover of membership and leadership.

—The developmental stage of adolescence that is characterized by rapid growth and change—physically, emotionally, intellectually, and socially. The adolescent's identity is often in a fluid state.

Student organizations must face these realities and develop organizational models and styles that capture the interest of a core of students who will make it a high priority. This would include being focused, being "where the action is," and being able to produce some visible results. Recruiting and developing leadership is another major issue. Bringing in freshmen and giving them essential and challenging tasks is one technique. An organizational structure that fosters the growth of varied types of leadership is essential. Setting realistic expectations and a clear focus is mandatory. But the central issue is again one of power. How can the student group be encouraged to assert the right of students to shape the major issues in school life rather than being a rubber stamp for the administration or being a body that focuses on the color of decorations at a dance rather than on disciplinary policy, quality of instruction, or the effects of contract negotiations. Adult advocates working with student groups can support their assertion of a significant role in decision making and of student-initiated and student-led activities.

Youth Advocates

Young people trained in the skills of case and class advocacy are another piece in the puzzle of making our systems serve people. In a few school districts,[12] young people are trained as advocates or ombudsmen to inform other students of their rights and provide assistance to other students—in cases of suspension, grading, corporal punishment, dress code, etc. Several questions arise. Should youth advocates be trained and supported by advocacy organizations within the school or independent of the school system? What is the source and scope of their power and authority? How can training and support services like legal counsel be funded?

Political Power: Age and Clout

At what age should young people be allowed to vote? The twenty-one-year limit was lowered to eighteen in 1971. Will young people have any significant power as long as they can't vote? Proponents argue that many young people, fifteen and over, are as well informed as most adults. They could choose to exercise their option but would not be obligated if they were disinterested or uncertain about how to vote. What better way to make government and history courses come alive than to have students participating in the voting process? Proponents insist that children and youth services will continue to be low priorities nationally as long as elected leaders are not accountable to young people.

Opponents of lowering the voting age point out that young people should not be burdened with that responsibility, that they should enjoy childhood while it lasts. Also, most young people usually don't pay taxes and are still the legal responsibilities of their parents. Others fear that young people could be easily influenced by propaganda and bribed by corrupt political machines.

One demographic fact is clear. The proportion of young people in America is decreasing while the relative proportion of people over sixty-five is increasing. This trend will continue. What are the political prospects for more equitable allocation of resources, especially publicly funded services, for children and their families if the proportionate number and political power of children and their families decrease? Is political power for young people essential for effective advocacy by children?

Power and rights for children and teenagers are frightening concepts to many adults. Many children are still being treated as property rather than precious human beings. Only recently have the courts clearly affirmed that children are full persons in the eyes of the law. Some young people are insisting that they be heard and are acting as advocates for each other. As one young man reflected: "I read my history books about the serfs, the slaves, and the suffragettes and realized: It's my turn

'The kids? Oh, they're fine. They're playing politics.'

now! All I ask of adults is listen to us, open some doors when we knock, and walk along side us as far as you can."

Notes

1. *New York—ex. rel. Wallace* v. *Lhotan.*
2. *In re Gault.*
3. *Planned Parenthood of Central Missouri* v. *Danforth.*
4. "Through the Eyes of Children," Massachusetts Department of Education, Boston, Massachusetts or contact Dr. Robert Sinclair, School of Education, University of Massachusetts, Amherst, Ma. 01002.
5. "Hearings on Incarcerated Children," videotape available from The Children's Express, 20 Charles Street, New York, NY 10014.
6. School district policy and the state law allowed corporal punishment to be administered only by the principal with prior parent permission. The Supreme Court, however, has ruled in a North Carolina case that corporal punishment by a teacher is legal under certain circumstances in North Carolina (*Baker* v. *Owen*, 395 F.

Supp. 294 (1975) affirmed at No. 75-279 U.S., October 20, 1975).

7. *Tinker et al.* v. *Des Moines Independent Community School District*, 393 U.S. 503 (1969).

8. *In re Gault,* 387 U. S. 1 (1967). See excerpts of the Supreme Court decision in chapter Two.

9. California has an excellent model recommended at the state level. Florida has another variant. Salt Lake City, Utah; Eugene, Oregon; and Lansing, Michigan have also developed models of decision making at the local school level.

10. National Coalition of Advocates for Students, 1501 18th Street, N.W., Washington, D.C., 20036.

11. The Youth Project, 1000 Wisconsin Ave., N.W., Washington, D.C. 20007.

12. Contact the National Commission on Resources for Youth that gathers information on youth projects in local communities (36 West 44th Street, New York, NY 10036).

CHAPTER EIGHT

A VISION AND AGENDA FOR CHILD ADVOCATES

Is the individual advocate a part of a social movement? Is there a child advocacy movement emerging with which the child advocate at the local level can unite?[1]

Signs of an Advocacy Movement

Some essential elements of a children's rights/child advocacy movement already exist. First, *rights* are being established as a basis for advocacy, especially since the 1967 *Gault* decision that said the rights of the U.S. Constitution apply to children as *persons* under the law. As chapter Two discussed, in the ten-year period following the 1967 *Gault* decision, a steady stream of court cases and legislation has laid a foundation for a new form of advocacy and also for further action in the courts and legislatures.

A second important ingredient is the development of *organizations* at the national, state and local levels that are focused on systems change rather than only case advocacy.

139

Many of these organizations identify themselves as advocacy groups and are forming alliances among themselves. The National Coalition of Advocates for Students is one example. At the national level, the Children's Defense Fund is an excellent example of an advocacy organization that focuses on some specific issues affecting children in all parts of the nation; it has also formed a Children's Public Policy Network to connect with state and local advocate groups.

The increasing number of *publications* that are becoming available is another sign of an emerging social movement. When I began teaching a course entitled "Advocacy for Children" at Temple University in 1974, only a few of the books listed in chapter Nine were in print. One notable and invaluable exception was *Child Advocacy: Report of a National (HEW) Baseline Study* by Alfred Kahn, Sheila Kammerman and Brenda McGowan, published in 1972. Chapter Nine lists some of the books, handbooks and audio-visual materials that are now available.

A fourth indication of a developing movement is the *skilled leadership* that is emerging at the national, state and local levels. Marian Wright Edelman of the Children's Defense Fund is probably the most widely known. At the local and state levels, Miriam Thompson of Advocates for Children in New York City, and Steve Bing of the Massachusetts Advocacy Center, and Gil Cisneras of the Colorado Children's Education Project have the savvy and skills to lead growing organizations and coalitions of advocacy groups. To date, the leadership has kept a relatively low profile. Most of the leadership keeps in close touch with the children they are serving. They spend most of their time "in the trenches" rather than leading media events.

Legal resources are more readily available to provide the legal backup needed for the advocacy movement. Nonprofit, public interest law centers have formed to provide individual and class action assistance, usually at no cost. For example, the National Juvenile Law Center operates out of St. Louis, Missouri, and has affiliate centers in other areas of the country.

A *focus* and *clearer definition of child advocacy* is emerging. Instead of being a vague, catch-all phrase referring to "anyone who did something for a child," a consensus is growing around the focus proposed by Kahn, Kammerman and McGowan in the HEW child advocacy study. Child advocacy must include class advocacy and systems change advocacy, and not just case advocacy for individual children being hurt by the system's policies, procedures or practices (or lack thereof). Child advocacy is intervention on behalf of children to see that systems serve rather than harm children. One-on-one, case advocacy is used as a first step toward system change.

Professional child advocates are being funded and hired in a few institutions and systems. Their role is to be advocates for children in hospitals, mental health systems, residential programs and prisons. Some staff members in child abuse prevention and treatment programs are called advocates. Many are nonlawyers. In addition, some lawyers now identify themselves as child advocates and represent the child in abuse, placement and custody cases. Staff persons working for advocacy organizations are also professional child advocates.

There has been *governmental support and recognition* of child advocacy as a developing movement. The National Center of Child Advocacy was established in 1972 in the Department of Health, Education and Welfare's Office of Child Development. Some child advocacy projects were funded in the 1970's as pilots or model programs. The Office of Juvenile Justice and Delinquency Prevention has funded youth advocacy projects based upon a systems change definition of advocacy. They require that youth be fully involved in the planning and implementation of the projects and that the advocacy organization be independent of the system being changed. Some states have also set up advocacy structures, usually for children with special needs like handicaps or mental illnesses.

What Is Needed?

Despite these beginnings, the child advocacy/children's rights movement is in the "infancy" stages. If it is to continue to develop, it needs to expand and intensify.

Child advocates need to form *alliances* with other power groups in American society. Finding common concerns with labor unions whose members' children are affected by systems like schools and juvenile justice is one resource. Public service employee unions should not be forgotten. Business leaders who see the short- and long-range effects of failing schools, rising juvenile delinquency and poor health care are valuable allies as part of change strategy. Religious organizations and other community organizations also need to be involved.

A *political base* that will provide political clout for substantive changes in institutions and systems and for legislation establishing comprehensive children's services is a must. Child advocates must elect sympathetic political leaders. Lobbying, by volunteers and by professional lobbyists, at all levels of the legislative process is vitally important. What can child advocates expect at the public policy level if the Pentagon has 300 paid lobbyists and advocacy organizations have five? I recognize that building a political base is difficult and time consuming. But it's a necessity.

We need advocacy *organizations* of all shapes and sizes. Some must focus on specific groups of children as does the Association for Children with Learning Disabilities. Others must concentrate on all children affected by a system, like the National Committee for Citizens in Education. Advocacy organizations at all three levels of decision making—local, state and federal—are needed. Some organizations will gather together and focus the energies of particular groups of advocates—the parents and/or children, institutional staffs and/or the professions, citizens and policymakers. Coalitions of those constituent groups can be formed around specific issues. Some advocacy organizations will need to be financially and politically independent of the systems they are changing, while other advocacy groups will be institutionally connected to the system they are influencing.

A *sense of identity* among child advocates needs to be heightened. Many people are working as child advocates but do not identify themselves as such or do not ally themselves with other child advocates. The tradition of individualism is strong in America. The emergence of advocacy organizations, leadership, and clearer definition of advocacy are factors that help shape a sense of identity. A first step for people who feel isolated in their local communities is to contact one or more of the national organizations listed in the Resource Section and use that contact to establish links to others with common concerns in other parts of the country and also use it to locate other advocates in your own community.

Money to carry out advocacy efforts is a major problem that must be faced. The advocacy movement needs a sound financial base. Forming and maintaining organizations that carry on sustained efforts to change systems like schools, juvenile justice and social services requires money. This is especially true for organizations that believe advocates must be independent (financially and structurally) from the system they are changing. From where will adequate funding come? Child advocates will need to begin by reaching into their own pockets for dues and then reaching out to other private and public sources. The political action committees (lobbying arms) of many labor unions raise over a million dollars a year to "advocate" their special interests in the state legislature. How much will be raised from child advocates each year to press the interests of children? Perhaps the traditional measure of church giving—the tithe, or ten percent of one's income—could be adjusted to one percent or two percent of one's yearly income as a starting point for individuals and groups.

Child advocates need clear *goals* to clarify what we want and where we are going. It's been said, "If you don't know where you're going, any path will do." Advocates need to set clear goals—one year, five years, ten years, so we can wisely select specific issues for immediate action. The goals need to be stated in specific, measurable terms, rather than vague generalities. (For example, see the goals for children's health that the Children's Defense Fund sets, pp. 145-46.)

Envisioning what is needed and where a children's rights/child advocacy movement is heading can be clarified by looking at a child advocacy system that has evolved in Denmark (see pp. 146-48).

Children's Defense Fund ten-year agenda for children

- Redirecting current child welfare policies and fiscal incentives which are anti-child, anti-family and geared toward discontinuous and expensive out-of-home care. Our goal is to ensure every child a home and a permanent, loving family—their own or an adoptive one.
- Ensuring every child access to basic primary and preventive health care. That 10 million American children receive no routine health care and 20 million have not been fully immunized against preventable diseases is not only a national disgrace, it is extremely costly.
- Providing access to flexible, quality child care for children whose mothers have to work or who have special needs because of handicap, poverty or temporary family crises.
- Diverting as many children as possible from a bogged-down and inadequate juvenile justice system through preventive services.
- Eliminating school exclusion practices that discriminate against children because they are "different," with the result that more than 1½ million school-age children are not being enrolled in school and millions more are growing up ignorant and functionally illiterate. Our goal is to ensure that every child receives an education that is fairly administered and appropriate to his or her needs.

These goals are not only critically important to millions of children, they are achievable and cost-effective. Preventive health services are not as expensive as untreated childhood illness. Education is not as expensive as ignorance. Services to families are far less expensive than the long-term results of family breakup.

Child Health (Fact Sheet from Children's Defense Fund)

The Problem

An estimated ten million American children get no regular primary health care. Half of all children under fifteen years of age have never been to a dentist. Twenty million children in the US are inadequately protected against basic diseases we know how to prevent: polio, diptheria, tetanus, whooping cough, measles, mumps, and rubella. Among some minority groups and in some rural areas, the infant mortality rates are like those of an underdeveloped nation. In our nation's capital, one in 33 nonwhite infants dies each year.

What most families need and want are routine health services—a place to go for care for earaches, sore throats, regular checkups, and immunizations. Our experience and research clearly indicate that if each child could be assured of a place to get these basic services, their lives would be significantly improved. Yet, it is in the area of primary health care where there are the most striking disparities in access to and quality of services received by the poor and the affluent. Too often it is ignored by policymakers and local planners, taking a back seat to topics like catastrophic illness and specialist care.

Immediate Goals

1. Enactment in this Congress of a strengthened Child Health Assessment Program (CHAP) which will expand and improve the Early and Periodic Screening, Diagnosis and Treatment Program (EPSDT) by assuring effective outreach; expanding Medicaid eligibility; broadening the scope of health services covered by Medicaid; developing mechanisms to assure that services get to needy children; encouraging participation by a wide range of qualified

providers; and strengthening states' capacity to deliver services to needy children.

2. Improving the administration of EPSDT, with or without CHAP, through needed regulatory changes; coordination between EPSDT and other federally-funded health programs; development of appropriate program goals, program improvement plans, and statistical reporting.

3. Development of a network of health advocates at the state and local level.

Longer-Range Goals

1. Improvement of existing federal programs which finance or provide child health services, including Maternal and Child and Crippled Children's Services (Title V of the Social Security Act) and Medicaid (Title XIX of the Social Security Act).

2. Legislation that will fund programs to promote the more effective delivery of health services, including expanded and improved support of neighborhood and community health centers, children and youth projects, primary care centers and HMOs.

3. Enactment of a sound program of comprehensive national health insurance.

Denmark's Advocacy System—A Model

A child advocacy system in Denmark that has evolved over the past seventy years offers a model of what does work and offers a vision of what could be adapted to this country. Marsden and Mary Wagner have lived in Denmark and studied the Danish system. They propose that:

> Program planners in the United States have alternatives besides conducting research that takes years to yield results or instituting untested programs. They can learn from other nations' experience. Denmark has had a nationwide multilevel

child-advocacy system since the turn of the century. This system has evolved over the decades through trial and error into a program for the support of children which has much to offer the rest of the world. In view of the urgency of the need, not to mention the expense of error, we might do well to examine in detail Denmark's experience.[2]

The essential features of the Danish advocacy system are:

1. The Child and Youth Committee (CYC) in each township is a permanent committee of the elected township council. The C.Y.C.'s membership is composed of a majority of the elected township council members (three of five, or four of seven) and two or three appointed citizens. All of the members are lay people rather than professionals. Since the C.Y.C. has a majority of elected township council members, it is rooted in the political system. The C.Y.C. has political policymaking power.

2. The C.Y.C. has a budget to hire a full-time professional staff to carry out the details and policy set by the C.Y.C.

3. A major function of the C.Y.C. is to provide *protection* for the child. There are clearly drawn guidelines to govern when the C.Y.C. can intervene on behalf of a child, especially in family problems. The C.Y.C. can intervene to protect the child and can provide supportive services to the family. The C.Y.C. removes a child from the family only as a last resort.

4. A second major function of the C.Y.C. is to promote the best living conditions for the child in the community. Thus, the C.Y.C. must see that schools, day-care centers, recreation centers, and residential facilities are provided and are monitored. In addition, the C.Y.C. reviews plans for apartment buildings, traffic patterns, public transportation facilities, and other community services to see that the needs of children are taken into account.

5. The C.Y.C. has not only the power to set policy and review and monitor, it has the *power of the purse*. For example, a day-care center can't be built or a new apartment building cannot be funded until the C.Y.C. gives its stamp of

approval. The C.Y.C. has power and authority both politically and fiscally.

6. There is a complex system of checks and balances and appeal procedures to protect the rights of the parents and the interests of other groups in the community. However, the C.Y.C. is mandated to put children's rights first—to be the clear advocate for the child.

7. The child advocacy system has evolved over a seventy-year period and it works. It has organically grown through trial and error, planning and revision. This is probably one of the most important points for the U.S.: the system works well as a model of what could be adapted to American society.

Yet, the differences between Denmark and the United States are significant. Denmark is the size of a small state and has only 5 million people (compared to our 225 million in the U.S.). Denmark's population is relatively homogenous racially and ethnically, and ninety-seven percent of the people belong to the Lutheran Church. There can not be a transplant of the Danish model to the United States, but it does offer a working model that gives child advocates in this country a vision of what can be done in a Western democratic society.

At present, most child advocates in the United States are working diligently and often alone in local communities, usually doing case advocacy. Will they join with others in advocacy organizations and an emerging child advocacy movement to develop and implement a nationwide child advocacy system? Will child advocates join together to forge more laws, support structures, and safeguards that will help create a public policy for our children that is as clear and well funded as our defense policy?

The 1980s will be a critical decade for America's children. A child born in 1979 will turn twenty-one in the year 2000. Thus the children of the 1980s will be the adults of the 21st century. Time does not wait for the growing child. Now is the time for child advocates to join together to forge public policy and

structures that guarantee rights, nurture, and choice for our nation's dearest resource.

Notes

1. See *The Children's Rights Movement*, edited by Beatrice and Ronald Gross (Anchor, 1977) for a collection of articles discussing these issues.

2. See Marsden and Mary Wagner, *The Danish National Child Care System*, Westview Press, (1898 Flatiron Court, Boulder, Colorado, 80301), 1966. See also the report of the Joint Commission on the Mental Health of Children, *Crisis in Child Mental Health*, where a national child advocacy system was proposed in 1960. One major problem with the proposal was lack of primary focus on the local community council with political and fiscal clout.

Child Advocacy Within the System by James Paul, G. Ronald Newfeld, and John W. Pelosi, editors (Syracuse University Press, 1977) is also a useful, focused resource.

CHAPTER NINE

ORGANIZATIONS AND RESOURCES

There are countless times when advocates in local communities need information that has probably already been gathered by others. Finding groups and organizations that are focused on an area of concern and that can offer information and support is an important fact-finding step.

Listed below are some national organizations that can help with facts, materials, advice and perhaps with training or technical assistance. The list is not all-inclusive but includes the groups with strong track records for data-gathering or action. Legal assistance groups are also included.

The Children's Public Policy Network at Children's Defense Fund (1520 New Hampshire Ave., N.W., Washington D.C. 20036, 202-483-1470) is probably the single best place to write or call.

Listed below are national organizations that may have relevant printed materials or audio-visual resources. But be sure to ask them for the names and addresses of groups and contacts in your area and state. Many of the national groups listed here have state and local chapters.

One additional resource that may be in your public library is the *National Children's Directory,* which lists children's groups by state and subject. (It is also available from Urban Information Interpreters, Inc., P. O. Box AH, College Park, Md., 20740.)

National Organizations

Action for Children's Television
46 Austin Street
Newtonville, MA 02160

Alexander Graham Bell Assoc. for the Deaf
3416 Volta Place, N.W.
Washington, D.C. 20007

American Academy of Pediatrics
1801 Hinman Avenue
Evanston, IL 60204

American Civil Liberties Union
22 East 40th Street
New York, NY 10016

American Coalition of Citizens with Disabilities
1346 Connecticut Avenue, N.W.
Suite 1124
Washington, D.C. 20036

American Friends Service Committee
1501 Cherry Street
Philadelphia, PA 19102

American Home Economics Assoc.
2010 Massachusetts Avenue, N.W.
Washington, D.C. 20036

American Humane Assoc.
5351 S. Roslyn Street
Englewood, CO 80111

Assoc. of Junior Leagues
Nat'l Child Advocacy Project
825 Third Avenue
New York, NY 10022

American Speech and Hearing Assoc.
10801 Rockville Pike
Rockville, MD 20852

Center on Human Policy
216 Ostrom Avenue
Syracuse, NY 13210

Center for Law and Education
Guttman Library
6 Appian Way
Cambridge, MA 02138

Closer Look Information Center for the Handicapped
P. O. Box 1492
Washington, D.C. 20013

Children's Defense Fund
1520 New Hampshire Avenue, N.W.
Washington, D.C. 20036

Child and Family Justice Project
Nat'l Council of Churches
475 Riverside Drive
Room 560
New York, NY 10027

Children's Foundation
1028 Connecticut Avenue,
N.W.
Washington, D.C. 20036

Child Welfare League of
America
67 Irving Place
New York, NY 10003

Church Women United in the
USA
475 Riverside Drive
Suite 812
New York, NY 10027

Council for Exceptional Children
1920 Association Drive
Reston, VA 22091

Day Care and Child Development Council of America
622 14th Street, N.W.
Washington, D.C. 20036

Designs for Change
220 S. State Street
Suite 1616
Chicago, IL 60604

Epilepsy Foundation of
America
1828 L Street, N.W.
Suite 405
Washington, D.C. 20036

League of Women Voters
1730 M Street, N.W.
Washington, D.C. 20036

Legal Services Corporation
733 15th Street, N.W.
Washington, D.C. 20036

Mental Health Assoc.
Nat'l Headquarters
1800 North Kent Street
Arlington, VA 22209

Mental Health Law Project
1220 Nineteenth Street, N.W.
Washington, D.C. 20036

Mexican-American Legal Defense Fund
28 Geary Street
San Francisco, CA 94108

Nat'l Assoc. for the Advancement of Colored People
1790 Broadway
New York, NY 10019

NAACP Legal Defense and
Educational Fund
10 Columbus Circle
New York, NY 10019

Nat'l Assoc. for the Deaf
Legal Defense Fund
Florida Avenue & 7th Street,
N.E.
Suite 311
Washington, D.C. 20002

Nat'l Assoc. for the Education
of Young Children
1834 Connecticut Avenue,
N.W.
Washington, D.C. 20009

Nat'l Assoc. for Children with Learning Disabilities
4156 Library Road
Pittsburgh, PA 15234

Nat'l Assoc. of the Deaf
814 Thayer Avenue
Silver Spring, MD 20910

Nat'l Assoc. for Retarded Citizens
2709 Avenue E East
P. O. Box 6109
Arlington, TX 76011

Nat'l Assoc. of Social Workers
1425 H Street, N.W.
Washington, D.C. 20005

Nat'l Black Child Development Institute
1463 Rhode Island Avenue, N.W.
Washington, D.C. 20005

Nat'l Center for Child Advocacy and the Children's Bureau
P.O. 1182
Washington, D.C. 20013

Nat'l Center for Law and the Handicapped
1235 N. Eddy Street
South Bend, IN 46617

Nat'l Coalition of ESEA Title 1 Parents
412 West 6th Street
Wilmington, DE 19801

Nat'l Commission on Resources for Youth
36 West 44th Street
New York, NY 10036

Nat'l Congress of Parents and Teachers
700 N. Bush Street
Chicago, IL 60611

Nat'l Council on Crime & Delinquency
Continental Plaza
411 Hackensack Avenue
Hackensack, NJ 07601

Nat'l Council of Jewish Women, Inc.
15 East 26th Street
8th floor
New York, NY 10010

Nat'l Council of Negro Women, Inc.
1346 Connecticut Avenue, N.W.
Washington, D.C. 20036

Nat'l Council of Organizations for Children and Youth
1910 K Street, N.W.
Room 404
Washington, D.C. 20006

Nat'l Easter Seal Society for Crippled Children and Adults
2023 W. Ogden Avenue
Chicago, IL 60612

Nat'l Federation of the Blind
1346 Connecticut Avenue,
  N.W.
Suite 212, Dupont Circle
  Bldg.
Washington, D.C. 20036

Nat'l Head Start Assoc.
c/o Community Teamwork,
  Inc.
10 Bridge Street
Lowell, MA 01852

Nat'l Juvenile Law Center
St. Louis University School of
  Law
3701 Lindell Boulevard
St. Louis, MO 63108

Nat'l Legal Aid and Defender
  Assoc.
1155 East 60th Street
Chicago, IL 60637

Nat'l Organization for
  Women
5 South Wabash
Suite 1615
Chicago, IL 60603

Nat'l Public Interest Research
  Group
1832 M Street, N.W.
Washington, D.C. 20036

Nat'l Rural Center
1828 L Street, N.W.
Suite 1000
Washington, D.C. 20036

Nat'l Student Volunteer Program Action
806 Connecticut Avenue,
  N.W.
Washington, D.C. 20006

Nat'l Society for Autistic
  Children
169 Tampa Avenue
Albany, NY 12208

Nat'l Urban Coalition
1201 Connecticut Avenue,
  N.W.
Washington, D.C. 20036

Nat'l Urban League
500 East 62nd Street
New York, NY 10021

Nat'l Youth Alternatives
  Project
1820 Connecticut Avenue,
  N.W.
Washington, D.C. 20009

Native American Rights
  Fund
1712 N Street, N.W.
Washington, D.C. 20036

North American Council on
  Adoptable Children
250 East Blaine
Riverside, CA 92507

Parents Anonymous
2009 Farrell Avenue
Redondo Beach, CA 90278

Parents Network, Nat'l Committee for Citizens in Education
Wilde Lake Village Green
Suite 410
Columbia, MD 21044

Parents Without Partners, Inc. (PWP)
Information Center
Suite 1000
7910 Woodmont Avenue
Washington, D.C. 20004

Puerto Rican Legal Defense and Educational Fund, Inc.
95 Madison Avenue
New York, NY 10016

Spina Bifida Assoc. of America
343 South Dearborn Street
Room 319
Chicago, IL 60604

United Cerebral Palsy Assoc.
66 East 34th Street
New York, NY 10016

U. S. Youth Council
1221 Connecticut Avenue, N.W.
Washington, D.C. 20036

Youth Liberation
2007 Washtenaw Avenue
Ann Arbor, MI 48104

Youth Project
1000 Wisconsin Avenue, N.W.
Washington, D.C. 20007

National Hot Lines

These toll-free hot lines are examples of some of the national hot lines. Others exist at the state level or in regions. Check your local telephone book or operator. Some telephones books now have a Guide to Human Services that list local numbers to call and special hotlines.

Most States have a Child Abuse Hotline—800-CHILD-LINE 923-0313

National Runaway Switchboard—800-621-4000

Parents Network—800-NETWORK (National Committee for Citizens in Education)

Children's Public Policy Network—800-424-9602 (Children's Defense Fund)

Books and Articles for Child Advocates

Brief descriptions of some of the best books are given below. Most are in paperback and are available from your library, bookstore or the address given.

American Civil Liberties Union (22 E. 40th St., New York, N.Y. 10016) publishes a series of handbooks that use a question-and-answer format to explain the law in language that non-lawyers can understand. These handbooks are "a must" for people working with youth. They are also appropriate for use in high school classrooms.

The Rights of Young People by Alan Sussman, 1976.

The Rights of Students by Alan Levine, 2nd edition.

Other handbooks in the series include *The Rights of Mental Patients, The Rights of Hospital Patients, The Rights of the Poor, The Rights of Prisoners, The Rights of Teachers.*

The Juvenile Rights Project of A.C.I.U. also published a monthly *Children's Rights Report,* which was an excellent resource. Funding difficulties have interfered with its regularity. Ask if it's available.

America's Children 1976, Coalition for Children and Youth, 1910 K Street, N.W., Washington, D.C. 20006. Provides facts about children and families in America in a very readable form, using many pie charts and graphs.

Biklen, Douglas. *Let Our Children Go: An Organizing Manual for Advocates and Parents* (Human Policy Press, P. O. Box 127, University Station, Syracuse, N.Y. 13210). This is an excellent resource for advocates working with handicapped children. It contains many specific examples and suggestions. Human Policy Press also has an especially well done and economical set of slide shows and posters and books for adults and children.

Burns, Marilyn. *I Am Not a Short Adult* (Little Brown, Boston, 1977). The book is for children and helps them explore how they feel about laws, rights, money and work.

Buskin, Martin. *Parent Power: A Candid Handbook for Dealing with Your Child's School* (Walker and Company, New York, 1975). Written for parents, especially those living in the suburbs. Discusses quality of a good school district: curriculum tests, special education, guidance counseling and citizen committees.

Children's Defense Fund publications are extensive and especially well researched and written (1520 New Hampshire Ave., N.W., Washington, D. C. 20036). Some of their major research studies are:

> *Children Out of School in America*
> *School Suspensions: Are They Helping Children?*
> *The Elementary and Secondary School Civil Rights Survey: An Analysis*
> *Doctors and Dollars Are Not Enough*
> *EPSDT: Does It Spell Health Care for Poor Children?*
> *Children in Adult Jails*
> *Children Without Homes: An Examination of Public Responsibility to Children in Out-of-Home Care*
> *Who Needs Child Care? Policy Options for the '80s*

Each one carefully documents the scope and nature of the problem and then discusses very specific policies and practices on which advocate groups can focus.

In addition to the research and proposals for change, C.D.F. also publishes many useful handbooks. An excellent one for parents is *Child Advocacy: It's Time to Stand Up for Your Child.* Others on specific topics include:

> *94-142 and 504: Numbers That Add Up to Educational Rights for Handicapped Children*
> *How Special Education Advocacy Can Work: A Mississippi Case Study*
> *Your School Records*
> *Misclassification: The Resegregation of Black Children in Public Schools*

Where Do You Look? Whom Do You Ask? How Do You Know?
  Resources for Child Advocates
Health Care for Children: Policies and Principles for Child
  Advocates
A Brief Guide to Children Without Homes
Federal Programs Affecting Children Without Homes
For the Welfare of Children
Title XX: Social Services in Your State
The Child Care Handbook
National Legislative Agenda for Children
A Portrait of Inequality: Black and White Children in America
America's Children and Families: A Profile
Children and the Federal Budget: What the President Proposes
A Child Advocate's Guide to Capitol Hill and Federal Agencies
Building a House on the Hill for Our Children

Cottle, Thomas, *Children in Jail: Seven Lessons in American Justice* (Beacon Press, Boston, 1977). Powerfully written stories of seven young people in jail whom Thomas Cottle visited and talked to over a period of several years. Hearing how these young people feel about themselves, their society, and their experience in our jails would be important reading for the person who wants to get involved or for a person who is jaded or tired.

Farson, Richard. *Birthrights* (Macmillan, New York, 1974). This book evokes discussion and stretches the reader to consider a far-reaching set of rights for children.

Forer, Lois. *No One Will Listen: How Our Legal Systems Brutalize the Youthful Poor.* (Grosset and Dunlap, New York, 1970). Judge Lois Forer writes from her experience and deep commitment as a juvenile court judge. She provides a careful description and analysis.

Gottlieb, David (ed.). *Children's Liberation* (Spectrum, 1973). This collection of six different articles on issues in children's rights is useful background reading.

Gross, Beatrice and Ronald (eds.). *The Children's Rights*

Movement (Anchor, 1977). Put this collection of articles on issues in children's rights at the top of your reading list. It provides background information and a variety of viewpoints by many advocates.

Harvard Educational Review. *The Rights of Children* (Harvard Educational Review, 1974). This paperback book contains articles by leading practitioners and scholars on significant children's issues like labeling, changing the juvenile justice system, use of drugs for treatment, and a history of children and the law.

Haskins, Jim. *Your Rights, Past and Present: A Guide for Young People* (Hawthorn Books, Inc., New York, 1977). Contains the history of children's rights and speaks specifically about labor, school, juvenile justice, rights at home, and the right to choose a home.

Holt, John. *Escape from Childhood: The Needs and Rights of Children* (Ballantine, New York, 1974). This is one of the most provocative books on children's rights and challenges its readers to consider the issues.

Inequality in Education, Special Issue on "Corporal Punishment in the Schools," Center for Law and Education, #23, Sept. 1978, (6 Appian Way, Cambridge, Mass. 02138). The articles in this special issue discuss *Ingraham* v. *Wright* and the effects of corporal punishment as a form of discipline in public schools.

Kahn, Alfred; Kammerman, Sheila; and McGowan, Brenda. *Child Advocacy: Report of a National Baseline Study* (Dept. H.E.W. Publication # (OCD) 7318). This federally funded study of the state of child advocacy in the early 1970s helped give sharper definition to the term and was an important step in focusing the plethora of activity that had been going on under the "child advocacy" banner.

Keniston, Kenneth. *All Our Children: The American Family Under Pressure*. (Harcourt Brace Jovanovich, New York, 1977). This report of the Carnegie Council on Children describes how government policy affects families in the United States. It has an excellent chapter on children and the law. In addition, there is an analysis of pressures affecting the American family and some fascinating proposals on economic, health and social service system changes that are needed.

The Children's Political Checklist (Denver Education Commission of the States, 1977). This was developed to help individuals and groups implement the recommendations from *All Our Children.* It's especially helpful for coalitions. Order from: Coalition for Children and Youth, 1910 K St., N.W., Washington, D.C. 20006.

Knitzer, Jane. "Child Advocacy: A Perspective," *American Journal of Orthopsychiatry*, 46 (2) (April, 1976), pp. 200-216. An excellent analysis and summary of child advocacy in 1976. It is briefer than the H.E.W. study, yet comprehensive.

Lindgren, Astrid. *Pippi Longstockings* (Penguin, 1950). This humorous children's book gives a view of children's rights through the child's eyes. It's great reading for adults and children—alone and together.

Making School Work: An Education Handbook for Students, Parents and Professionals. Available from Massachusetts Advocacy Center, 2 Park Square, Boston, Massachusetts 02116. $3.95. The question-and-answer format covers topics like school attendance, discipline, fees. Title I, special education, kinder- garten, lunches, tracking and school records. It is written for Massachusetts, but contains ideas and facts that are useful for parents in other states.

National Committee for Citizens in Education (Suite 410, Wilde Lake Village Green, Columbia, MD., 21044) has a series of handbooks that are very useful for citizens and parents concerned about public schools. They are very readable, concise and specific in addition to being inexpensive.

"On Being a Child," *Church and Society* (November-December, 1977, Presbyterian Church in the U.S. and United Presbyteri- an Church in the U.S.A.). This issue "On Being a Child" is an extensive report prepared for the General Assembly of the

United Presbyterian Church on the needs and rights of children. A study guide and bibliography are included. Order from: Church and Society, Room 1244K, 475 Riverside Drive, New York, N.Y. 10027.

> *Developing Leadership for Parent/Citizen Groups*
> *Parents Organizing to Improve Schools*
> *Los Padres Se Organizan Para Mejorar Las Escuelas*
> *Fundraising by Parent/Citizen Groups*
> *The Rights of Parents in the Education of Their Children*
> *Who Controls the Schools?*
> *Collective Bargaining and Teacher Strikes*
> *School Budgets—You Can Understand Them and Influence Them*
> *School Based Management—New Fad or New Force?*
> *Violence in Our Schools: What to Know About It, What to Do About It*

Paul, et al. *Child Advocacy Within the System* (Syracuse University Press, 1977). This is an excellent book for professionals working within a system.

Richette, Lisa. *Throwaway Children* (Delta, 1969). On the basis of her experience in juvenile court, Judge Lisa Richette has written a vivid, hard-hitting account of the brutality that many children experience.

Seen, Milton E. *Speaking Out for America's Children* (Yale University Press, 1977). Brief quotations and reflections from America's leading child advocates are collected by Dr. Seen. Basic reading for all advocates.

Schimmel, David, and Fischer, Louis. *The Rights of Parents, 1977*. Available from National Committee for Citizens in Education, Suite 410, Wilde Lake Village Green, Columbia, MD 21044. This provides a clear explanation of some rights that parents have. In addition, some of the important cases are included in the Appendix.

Tool Catalog. Washington, D.C.: American Association of University Women, 1972, AAUW Sales Office, 2401 Virginia Ave., N.W. Washington, D.C. 20037. An easy-to-use book of techniques to help groups effect change in their communities. The contents are divided into six parts: action guidelines, dealing with institutions, demonstrations of support and opposition, fact finding, information and publicity techniques, and organization and planning.

Wagner, Marsten, and Wagner, Mary. "Child Advocacy in Denmark," Chapter 1 in *The Danish National Child Care System* (Westview Press, Boulder, Col., 1976). The Danish child advocacy system is fully described by the Wagners who also discuss other components of the child care system.

Westman, Jack. *Child Advocacy: New Professional Roles for Helping Families* (The Free Press, New York, 1979 (hard cover)). This is a lengthy and thorough discussion of advocacy issues in schools, the legal system, social services, health care and mental health care. A chapter focuses on each field.

Wilkerson, Albert (ed.). *The Rights of Children: Emergent Concepts in Law and Society* (Temple University Press, Philadelphia, 1973 (hard cover)). Some of the complexities and technical issues in children's rights are discussed by several experts.

Wooten, Kenneth. *Weeping in the Playtime of Others: America's Incarcerated Children* (McGraw Hill, New York, 1976). Powerfully written, this investigation and analysis into the juvenile justice system lets you hear and feel the "weeping of children," but also documents the way the political and economic systems make it very resistant to change. Highly recommended.

Youth Liberation Press, *Young People and the Law* (3rd Edition, 2007 Washtenaw Ave., Ann Arbor, Michigan, 48104, 1978). Written by young people for young people, this booklet has cartoons and a style that would appeal to all types of teenagers. It explains the law carefully, but in an interesting format.

ACKNOWLEDGMENTS

The publisher wishes to express appreciation for permission to reprint the following material.

"Becoming Involved," a speech by Gerri Chester. Originally printed in *Network,* a publication of the National Committee for Citizens in Education. Used by permission of *Network.*

Cartoons by Tony Auth originally appeared in *The Philadelphia Inquirer.* Copyright © 1973, 1975, 1976, 1977 by *The Philadelphia Inquirer.* Reprinted by permission of Tony Auth and *The Philadelphia Inquirer.*

Material developed by The Children's Defense Fund (ten-year agenda for children and fact sheet on child health).

Excerpts from *Escape From Childhood: The Needs & Rights of Children,* by John Holt (New York: E.P. Dutton, 1974). Copyright © 1974 by John Holt. Used by permission.

Excerpts from "Floyd Logan: A Lifetime Devoted to a Cause," by Helen Oakes. *The Oakes Newsletter* (Philadelphia, Pa.), vol. VI, no. 5, January 28, 1975. Reprinted by permission.

"Ingredients For Effective Advocacy Groups." Adapted from materials developed by Don Moore and Ularsee Maner of Designs for Change (Chicago) as part of the School Advocacy Study.

Excerpts from *Let Our Children Go: An Organizing Manual for Advocates and Parents,* by Douglas Biklen. The Human Policy Press, P.O. Box 127, Syracuse, N.Y. 13210.

Excerpts from *Our Kindly Parent . . . The State,* by Patrick T. Murphy (New York: Penguin Books, 1977). Copyright © 1977 by Patrick Murphy. Used by permission.

Material developed by Parents' Union (Vera Simon case, and two special education cases illustrating Parents' Union procedures).